Personhood

Other Books of Related Interest

Opposing Viewpoints Series

Artificial Intelligence and the Technological Singularity
DNA Testing and Privacy
Immigration Bans
Virtual Reality

At Issue Series

Ethical Pet Ownership
Political Corruption
Reproductive Rights
The Right to a Living Wage

Current Controversies Series

Deporting Immigrants
Genetic Engineering
Learned Helplessness, Welfare, and the Poverty Cycle
The Political Elite and Special Interests

"Congress shall make no law ... abridging the freedom of speech, or of the press."

First Amendment to the US Constitution

The basic foundation of our democracy is the First Amendment guarantee of freedom of expression. The Opposing Viewpoints series is dedicated to the concept of this basic freedom and the idea that it is more important to practice it than to enshrine it.

OPPOSING
VIEWPOINTS®
SERIES

Personhood

Gary Wiener, Book Editor

GREENHAVEN
PUBLISHING

Published in 2022 by Greenhaven Publishing, LLC
353 3rd Avenue, Suite 255, New York, NY 10010

Copyright © 2022 by Greenhaven Publishing, LLC

First Edition

Articles in Greenhaven Publishing anthologies are often edited for length to meet page
requirements. In addition, original titles of these works are changed to clearly present
the main thesis and to explicitly indicate the author's opinion. Every effort is made to
ensure that Greenhaven Publishing accurately reflects the original intent of the authors.
Every effort has been made to trace the owners of the copyrighted material.

Cover image: Monkey Business Images/Shutterstock.com

Library of Congress Cataloging-in-Publication Data

Names: Wiener, Gary, editor.
Title: Personhood / Gary Wiener, book editor.
Description: First edition. | New York : Greenhaven Publishing, 2022. |
Series: Opposing viewpoints | Includes bibliographical references and index. | Audience:
Ages 15+ | Audience: Grades 10–12 | Summary: "Anthology of diverse viewpoints
exploring the scope of personhood regarding human slavery, right to life and right to end
life, animal rights, bioethics, corporate rights, and theology."—Provided by publisher.
Identifiers: LCCN 2020050958 | ISBN 9781534507654 (library
binding) | ISBN 9781534507630 (paperback)
Subjects: LCSH: Philosophical anthropology. | Humanism. | Persons.
Classification: LCC BD450 .P46219145 2022 | DDC 128—dc23
LC record available at https://lccn.loc.gov/2020050958

Manufactured in the United States of America

Website: http://greenhavenpublishing.com

Contents

Chapter 3: When Does Personhood Begin and End?

Chapter 4: Could Artificial Intelligence Attain Personhood?

The Importance of Opposing Viewpoints

Perhaps every generation experiences a period in time in which the populace seems especially polarized, starkly divided on the important issues of the day and gravitating toward the far ends of the political spectrum and away from a consensus-facilitating middle ground. The world that today's students are growing up in and that they will soon enter into as active and engaged citizens is deeply fragmented in just this way. Issues relating to terrorism, immigration, women's rights, minority rights, race relations, health care, taxation, wealth and poverty, the environment, policing, military intervention, the proper role of government—in some ways, perennial issues that are freshly and uniquely urgent and vital with each new generation—are currently roiling the world.

If we are to foster a knowledgeable, responsible, active, and engaged citizenry among today's youth, we must provide them with the intellectual, interpretive, and critical-thinking tools and experience necessary to make sense of the world around them and of the all-important debates and arguments that inform it. After all, the outcome of these debates will in large measure determine the future course, prospects, and outcomes of the world and its peoples, particularly its youth. If they are to become successful members of society and productive and informed citizens, students need to learn how to evaluate the strengths and weaknesses of someone else's arguments, how to sift fact from opinion and fallacy, and how to test the relative merits and validity of their own opinions against the known facts and the best possible available information. The landmark series Opposing Viewpoints has been providing students with just such critical-thinking skills and exposure to the debates surrounding society's most urgent contemporary issues for many years, and it continues to serve this essential role with undiminished commitment, care, and rigor.

The key to the series's success in achieving its goal of sharpening students' critical-thinking and analytic skills resides in its title—

Opposing Viewpoints. In every intriguing, compelling, and engaging volume of this series, readers are presented with the widest possible spectrum of distinct viewpoints, expert opinions, and informed argumentation and commentary, supplied by some of today's leading academics, thinkers, analysts, politicians, policy makers, economists, activists, change agents, and advocates. Every opinion and argument anthologized here is presented objectively and accorded respect. There is no editorializing in any introductory text or in the arrangement and order of the pieces. No piece is included as a "straw man," an easy ideological target for cheap point-scoring. As wide and inclusive a range of viewpoints as possible is offered, with no privileging of one particular political ideology or cultural perspective over another. It is left to each individual reader to evaluate the relative merits of each argument— as he or she sees it, and with the use of ever-growing critical-thinking skills—and grapple with his or her own assumptions, beliefs, and perspectives to determine how convincing or successful any given argument is and how the reader's own stance on the issue may be modified or altered in response to it.

This process is facilitated and supported by volume, chapter, and selection introductions that provide readers with the essential context they need to begin engaging with the spotlighted issues, with the debates surrounding them, and with their own perhaps shifting or nascent opinions on them. In addition, guided reading and discussion questions encourage readers to determine the authors' point of view and purpose, interrogate and analyze the various arguments and their rhetoric and structure, evaluate the arguments' strengths and weaknesses, test their claims against available facts and evidence, judge the validity of the reasoning, and bring into clearer, sharper focus the reader's own beliefs and conclusions and how they may differ from or align with those in the collection or those of their classmates.

Research has shown that reading comprehension skills improve dramatically when students are provided with compelling, intriguing, and relevant "discussable" texts. The subject matter of these collections could not be more compelling, intriguing, or urgently relevant to today's students and the world they are poised to inherit. The anthologized articles and the reading and discussion questions that are included with them also provide the basis for stimulating, lively, and passionate classroom debates. Students who are compelled to anticipate objections to their own argument and identify the flaws in those of an opponent read more carefully, think more critically, and steep themselves in relevant context, facts, and information more thoroughly. In short, using discussable text of the kind provided by every single volume in the Opposing Viewpoints series encourages close reading, facilitates reading comprehension, fosters research, strengthens critical thinking, and greatly enlivens and energizes classroom discussion and participation. The entire learning process is deepened, extended, and strengthened.

For all of these reasons, Opposing Viewpoints continues to be exactly the right resource at exactly the right time—when we most need to provide readers with the critical-thinking tools and skills that will not only serve them well in school but also in their careers and their daily lives as decision-making family members, community members, and citizens. This series encourages respectful engagement with and analysis of opposing viewpoints and fosters a resulting increase in the strength and rigor of one's own opinions and stances. As such, it helps make readers "future ready," and that readiness will pay rich dividends for the readers themselves, for the citizenry, for our society, and for the world at large.

Introduction

> *"The fact that the human being can*
> *have the representation 'I' raises him*
> *infinitely above all the other beings*
> *on earth. By this he is a person …*
> *that is, a being altogether different*
> *in rank and dignity from things,*
> *such as irrational animals, with*
> *which one may deal and dispose at*
> *one's discretion."*
>
> *—Immanuel Kant, 1798*

What is a person? The answer might be unexpectedly complicated. The concept of personhood has always been difficult to define. As one scholar writes, "*Personhood* is a fluid analytical term with diverse and debated meanings. It is often hard to discern who is considered to be a person, what being a person entails, or how this differs from having selfhood, or being an individual. Certain scholars have attempted to elucidate these terms; nevertheless, they are frequently used interchangeably."[1]

The stakes are high when it comes to acknowledging someone's or something's personhood. There are legal, moral, and ethical ramifications that go far beyond the simple act of granting—or limiting—personhood. Defining personhood is controversial in fields such as philosophy and law. It may be used to grant someone citizenship, equality, and liberty. As David L. Perry writes, "To be classified as a 'person' normally entails having strong moral rights and legal protections, and higher moral status than living things that cannot credibly be classified as persons."[2]

Traditionally, personhood has been a narrowly defined concept. For centuries, only human beings were recognized as viable persons in the eyes of the law. But even this concept was narrowly interpreted. In many countries, only white male landholders qualified for true personhood status. For example, in early nineteenth-century Great Britain, only the owners of substantial parcels of land were able to fully participate in the electoral process. It took reform bills of 1832, 1867, and 1884 to grant voting rights to more and more men. Even so, as in the United States, women and minorities need not have applied.

In the United States, a compromise of 1787 gave enslaved people the status of three-fifths of a white person. The Supreme Court's infamous *Dred Scott* decision of 1857, just a few years before the start of the US Civil War, ruled that enslaved people who had been freed were excluded from US citizenship and thus did not have legal rights. Though the Fourteenth Amendment of 1868 finally granted people of color the right to citizenship, it was not until the Voting Rights Act of 1964 that all African Americans gained the right to vote. Worse still, today those rights are being slowly eroded.

Women's rights came almost as slowly. Although women's suffrage movements were prominent in the United States since the mid 1800s, it was not until the ratification of the Nineteenth Amendment in 1920 that women were able to exercise their right to choose America's leaders. With all American human beings having at least a measure of personhood, the debate has evolved to consider the personhood status of non-human entities.

Times—and definitions—have changed. Now, a concept that once did not even apply to all persons has been expanded to include numerous non-human entities. In the attempt to support their causes, various groups have advocated for personhood for the unborn, for artificially intelligent beings such as robots and androids, and even for natural objects such as trees, rivers, and lakes. This broader understanding of the nature of personhood has raised numerous legal issues. According to law professor Lawrence

Solum, some of these include: "Are the unborn human persons? What is the difference between legal and moral personhood? What does it mean to say that a corporation is a legal person? Do the most intelligent animals deserve the rights of moral or legal persons?"[3]

As such questions suggest, court cases worldwide are currently being litigated to decide the personhood status of inanimate objects and non-human entities. In one prominent case in the United States, the entity won. In *Citizens United v. Federal Election Commission* the Supreme Court considered corporate personhood status—the notion that not just humans, but businesses as well, should be granted freedom of speech. But it wasn't just speech that was involved. The real aim of *Citizens United* was, as it is in so many cases, financial. The Supreme Court's decision favoring corporations, unions, and associations freed these groups to spend vast sums of money on political candidates. This led to the creation of what we now know as Super-PACs, groups of like-minded citizens who bond together in support of candidates and causes. Supporters of *Citizens United* consider the 5-4 Supreme Court decision a win for freedom of speech. Opponents believe that it increasingly enables the corruption of the American political system.

While American corporations have achieved a measure of personhood, debates about the personhood of many other non-human entities rage on. In an article for *Slate* magazine, Rachel Withers examines one thorny issue:

> In 2015, an A.I.-powered Twitter bot did something a little out there—avant-garde, one might say. It tweeted, "I seriously want to kill people," and mentioned a fashion event in Amsterdam. Dutch police questioned the owner of the bot over the death threat, claiming he was legally responsible for its actions, because it was in his name and composed tweets based on his own Twitter account.[4]

The question of responsibility for the threatening tweet is not as clear-cut as it might seem. Withers explains that if a proposed European Union law is enacted that grants personhood to AI, legal responsibility may lie with the bot itself. But can the law really blame artificial intelligence for the perceived threat? One may argue that because the tweet was sent out by an artificially intelligent bot, there was no real threat. But the possibility of what Withers calls "autonomous robo-harm" is no longer science fiction. What happens when a self-driven car loses control and plows into a sidewalk full of pedestrians?

The proposal for AI personhood has been criticized by over 150 experts in the fields of robotics, law, medicine, and ethics. They believe that AI personhood, as proposed, is nonsensical and impractical. As of now, the European Union has not decided what to do about AI personhood. But there can be no doubt that someone—or something—will have to be held responsible for the actions of artificially intelligent entities.

Another area that has seen hot debate is environmental personhood. The genesis of legal rights for nature arguments can be traced back to a 1972 scholarly article by Christopher D. Stone entitled, "Should Trees Have Standing—Toward Legal Rights for Natural Objects." In this essay, Stone acknowledges that "each time there is a movement to confer rights onto some new 'entity,' the proposal is bound to sound odd or frightening or laughable."[5] Nevertheless, in a well-reasoned essay, Stone observes, "It is not inevitable, nor is it wise, that natural objects should have no rights to seek redress in their own behalf. It is no answer to say that streams and forests cannot have standing because streams and forests cannot speak. Corporations cannot speak either; nor can states, estates, infants, incompetents, municipalities or universities."[6]

Stone's argument received a boost when Supreme Court justice William O. Douglas cited his defense of ecological personhood in a famous dissent in the case of *Sierra Club v. Morton* later the same year. The Sierra Club lost in its attempt to block the development of a ski resort in the Sierra Nevada, but the groundwork for environmental personhood was laid down. Given the conservative majority of the Supreme Court in recent years, the notion of environmental personhood has not fared well in the United States, but other countries have implemented measures to ensure the rights of natural objects. Such efforts are often led by indigenous peoples.

In 2007, for example, Ecuador recognized the legal rights of Pachamama, or Mother Earth. The effort was led by a native group, the National Confederation of Indigenous Nationalities of Ecuador. Ecuador, according to writer and activist Sanket Khandelwal, "became the first country ever to recognize and enshrine rights of nature within its Constitution."[7] In 2010, the Bolivian government followed suit, adopting the "Law of the Rights of Mother Earth."

In New Zealand, the adoption of protections for nature was also spearheaded by a tribal group. In 2014, urged on by the Maori indigenous people, the revered Whanganui River was accorded "legal status as a living entity."[8] Undoubtedly more countries will follow in the footsteps of these three trailblazers. With climate change posing an existential threat to Earth, legal personhood has emerged as a promising environmental strategy.

Opposing Viewpoints: Personhood presents a wide range of viewpoints that define and debate various concepts of personhood. In chapters titled "What Is Personhood?," "How Can Corporations Be Persons?," "When Does Personhood Begin and End?," and "Could Artificial Intelligence Attain Personhood?," authors discuss personhood's many uses and abuses in contemporary society, and they contemplate the logic of applying the personhood—legal, moral, theological, and constitutional—to the diverse entities that are now being placed under its umbrella. These entities include the elderly, fetuses, nature, corporations, and artificial intelligence. The viewpoints that follow demonstrate that our understanding of personhood is still emerging in the twenty-first century world and that the history of its use in everyday life is still being written.

Endnotes

1. Dafna Shir-Vertesh, "Personhood," Oxford Bibliographies, February 28, 2017. https://www.oxfordbibliographies.com/view/document/obo-9780199766567 /obo-9780199766567-0169.xml

2. David L. Perry, "Ethics and Personhood," Markkula Center for Applied Ethics, December 11, 2001. https://www.scu.edu/ethics/focus-areas/bioethics/resources /ethics-and-personhood/

3. Lawrence Solum, "Legal Theory Lexicon: Persons and Personhood," Legal Theory Blog, December 31, 2017. https://lsolum.typepad.com/legaltheory/2017/12/legal -theory-lexicon-persons-and-personhood.html

4. Rachel Withers, "The EU Is Trying to Decide Whether to Grant Robots Personhood," Slate, April 7, 2018. https://slate.com/technology/2018/04/the-eu-is-trying-to -decide-whether-to-grant-robots-personhood.html

5. Christopher D. Stone, "Should Trees Have Standing—Toward Legal Rights for Natural Objects," Southern California Law Review, 45, 1972, pp. 450–501. https://iseethics .files.wordpress.com/2013/02/stone-christopher-d-should-trees-have-standing.pdf

6. Christopher D. Stone, "Should Trees Have Standing—Toward Legal Rights for Natural Objects," Southern California Law Review, 45, 1972, pp. 450–501. https://iseethics .files.wordpress.com/2013/02/stone-christopher-d-should-trees-have-standing.pdf

7. Sanket Khandelwal, "Environmental Personhood: Recent Developments and the Road Ahead," Jurist, April 24, 2020. https://www.jurist.org/commentary/2020/04/ sanket-khandelwal-environment-person/

8. Sanket Khandelwal, "Environmental Personhood: Recent Developments and the Road Ahead," Jurist, April 24, 2020. https://www.jurist.org/commentary/2020/04 /sanket-khandelwal-environment-person/

CHAPTER 1

What Is Personhood?

Chapter Preface

Defining personhood would seem at first glance an easy task. A traditional definition of a "person" would read something like this: a human being regarded as an individual. And yet, in the early twenty-first century, the concept of personhood is being continually expanded. Common court cases now consider the notion of personhood for the unborn, personhood for corporations, personhood for robots, and personhood for nature. Are human rights becoming endangered as a result of extending personhood to non-humans? It is a valid question.

It is a mark of how quickly society advances that many humans did not enjoy full personhood until the twentieth century, and yet, in the twenty-first, personhood for non-humans has become a valid concept. It may be argued that society is considering granting personhood to non-humans even before all humans enjoy that designation. It is clear that disenfranchised members of society (those unable to vote), victims of human trafficking, and women in many countries worldwide do not enjoy the full benefits of personhood. Yet attorneys are in court at this very moment in history arguing that robots should be accorded legal personhood. We live in strange times.

While it is true that no attorney is arguing that robots be accorded the right to vote, it should be a reasonable goal to grant every human being on earth the full benefits of legal personhood before granting them to non-humans. But money and power often outweigh human rights, even in the best of nations. In the worst of nations, few citizens actually enjoy full personhood. Systemic racism, rigged elections, and other societal evils still limit the personhood of many on this planet.

When we grant personhood to non-humans, are we really giving rights to that entity, or are we actually limiting human behavior? Verlyn Klinkenborg cites a law that banned grizzly bears from a Wyoming county in the early 2000s. "The resolution made it seem as though grizzlies might somehow become aware of the ban and choose to obey or disobey it."[1] The real goal of such laws is to shape human behavior, Klinkenborg writes, not that of animals. How do we restrain human behavior so that animals are allowed to flourish?

The same is true of all attempts to bestow personhood on an aggrieved group in order to ameliorate their situation. Bestowing a title on the unborn, or nature, or the aging, isn't necessarily going to alter the behavior of those who are bent on continuing abusive behavior, especially if that behavior has a profit motive.

Nevertheless, bestowing personhood can have powerful effects on human behavior. As Tamara R. Piety argues in a paper entitled "Personhood Matters," personhood is a powerful metaphor. "Metaphors are important," she writes. "They may have powerful psychological impacts. This insight drives much of politics, advertising, and public relations—all of which seek to persuade."[2] Persuasion is the key here, Piety believes. Laws, and the interpretation of laws, are based on the ability to persuade others. In this regard, the idea of personhood can be a powerful ally in achieving justice for marginalized groups.

Endnotes

1. Verlyn Klinkenborg, "Animal 'Personhood': Muddled Alternative to Real Protection," Yale Environment 360, January 30, 2014. https://e360.yale.edu/features/animal_personhood_muddled_alternative_to_real_protection
2. Tamara R. Piety, "Personhood Matters," TU Law Digital Commons. https://digitalcommons.law.utulsa.edu/cgi/viewcontent.cgi?article=1478&context=fac_pub

> *"We ourselves, as biologically distinct creatures, have defined personhood, and to the best of our knowledge, no other being within any discussion of evolution has done so."*

Defining Personhood Is Complicated

Jean Lee

In the following viewpoint, Jean Lee explores humankind's origins and the philosophies and religious beliefs that serve to define the human condition. Lee traces humanity back to its earliest roots, examining how human beings evolved from lower species into their present form. She looks at how various religions define personhood, especially in terms of body and soul. And she suggests how the concept of personhood has become even more complex in the current age, both in legal terms and in practical ones. Jean Lee is a freelance writer working at the University of California, Berkeley.

As you read, consider the following questions:

1. What is the concept of "mosaic evolution"?
2. How is the concept of "soul" intrinsic to religious ideas about personhood?
3. Why is the concept of personhood "personal"?

"Defining Personhood," by Jean Lee, *Journal of Young Investigators*, March 23, 2002. https://www.jyi.org/2002-march/2002/3/23/defining-personhood. Licensed under CC BY 4.0 International.

Let us begin a philosophical exploration of the state of being a person, or "personhood." What specific attribution, qualification, or perspective defines personhood? In order to even begin discussing a question of this magnitude, we must agree that, first and foremost, there is no single, comprehensive definition of "person." A sense of awe may surround this question, or a sense of controversy. While acknowledging the controversy, let us venture forth and scratch the surface of this topic, exploring some ideas about personhood as expressed in various disciplines of study.

The Personhood of *Homo Sapiens*

At present, an estimated 6 billion human individuals exist on this planet. On Earth, humans—that is, people—have decidedly established themselves as a dominant population. While humans are not the most prevalent population (the number of arthropods is near 10^{18} individuals), they are the most dominant population in terms of influence upon the planet. Humans are dynamic and social; persons, people, and nations are ethnically and biologically diverse and highly developed, culturally and linguistically. One of the earliest proposed persons found by anthropologists, named Lucy, is an *Australopithecus afarensis*. She is surmised to be an important hominid link within human evolution. Present day humans are presumed to be a result of mosaic evolution; that is, our evolution was not purposeful, but random.

The ancestral primate that began the Primate order is placed in the tree of life at about 60 million years ago. According to evolutionary theory, human beings are not a culmination, but merely a continuance of the development of life that began with the "primordial soup" of ancient Earth atmospheres. The very elements constituting our bodies, passed through time as mass and energy, are ultimately guessed to be of interstellar origin. The famous Miller experiment demonstrated the "primordial formation" of amino acids (the building blocks of life) from a chemical reaction of water, methane, ammonia, and hydrogen. However, it can be held that "personhood" is a contemporary concept (philosophical, semantic, and linguistically variable), and not really a part of a scientific progression in itself. Perhaps the evolutionary theory of human emergence and taxonomic classifications has bearing on our interpretation of the concept, or perhaps it does not, especially in the here and now. We ourselves, as biologically distinct creatures, have defined personhood, and to the best of our knowledge, no other being within any discussion of evolution has done so.

The human brain is the largest and most complex living organ, a phenomenal apparatus that studies and evaluates even itself. What we might lack in physical ability as organisms, we make up for in mental capacity. We have a significant influence on Earth's biodiversity, habitats, and atmosphere. In the light of our search for personhood however, these scientific explorations explain only the physical dynamics of a human organism within the world. There is more to being a human—or so many of us have suggested.

Humanity and Spiritual Doctrine

Personhood may equate to what we call "humanity" as an individual or collective character trait. A dictionary yields the following definitions: a *person* is a living human, and an individual with character and personality. A person is manifested bodily and is unique. So far, we have examined the bodily manifestation. Let us peek into a little of what other key realms of study have to say about our character and personality components.

Complementing or confusing our understanding of science are the designs of our personal beliefs and religious doctrines. These deal with ethical and moral issues surrounding existence and purpose. One example is the monotheistic religion of Islam, in which surrender, submission, and service to God construct the moral character and way of life. In the Buddhist attitude of mind, a person is his or her own master of existence, capable of putting aside hindrances to reach the Enlightened State, in which the world no longer entangles his or her person. Ethical and moral viewpoints often step in when one must make a decision based upon one's understanding of scientific—as well as religious (that is, personal)—

knowledge and/or beliefs. In the fascinating work *On Monsters and Marvels*, Renaissance surgeon Ambroise Pare evaluates what modern medicine calls teratogenesis—the origins or causes of birth defects. He proposes an ominous list of 13 causes of malformed persons, which include the "wrath of God" and "demons and devils," in addition to "heredity or accidental illnesses." According to Pare, causes of birth defects range from moral failure to physical mishap in the human existence. The origin of birth defects is linked closely to the origin of birth itself. Where does Man originate? What is his purpose? How does one understand malformed infants not only scientifically, but also personally? Indeed the things of this physical world may be confounding enough; science participates in formulating possible answers, but so does personal doctrine. It is a constant struggle, in which one may try to separate personal biases from the practice of science, or choose to unite the two dominions as a common tool. Both involve a rich and perpetual exploration.

In addition to the many possible moral aspects of defining a person, a rich abundance of religious discourse, text and culture talk about the existence of the soul as being a defining element of personhood. Death is an inevitable boundary that all persons must cross; according to most religions and according to biological feasibility, personhood clearly includes a point of birth and of death. What will we do before we die? What will we do after we die? Let us examine a few spiritual or religious dictates briefly.

The Qur'an dictates that the human being is inseparably body and soul. In Hindu philosophy, as found in the *Taittiriya Upanishad*, there is a complete five-soul system under a Supreme Soul, called atman. In order to explore the state of being human and to develop spiritually, different levels of human consciousness can be reached with practice and devotion, especially those beyond the immediate physical world. According to Judeo-Christian belief, the first man—Adam—is formed by God the Creator "from the dust of the ground" (*NIV translation*). In Genesis, God bestows the soul of the first man—and thus all humans—by breathing into his nostrils the "breath of life." In an overwhelming number of religions, there is clearly a physical nature but also a spiritual nature to human beings. This is also true of ancient Egyptian beliefs, which held that a person is composed of at least four factions, the *ka* (vital force), *ba* (consciousness), *akh* (psyche), and *ab* (heart and deep nature), working within the corporeal and spiritual person during and after life.

Individual Opinions and Definition

In order to establish what individuals' opinions and definitions are about personhood, 86 university students from diverse ethnic and religious backgrounds were surveyed. Sixty-eight believed that a human being could be considered a person "at birth." Twenty-nine students believed that a person exists when the fetus achieves the beginnings of brain function in utero (around the sixth gestational month), 18 indicated the instant of fertilization signified existence, and 15 chose "sometime during fetal development before birth" as the critical point. Others didn't know or didn't want to answer. More than half of the students declared that a clinically brain-dead individual is still a person; about one-fourth of the surveyed students stated that this individual is not a person any longer. An overwhelming 75.5% of the students proclaimed that people have souls. Following up on this question, the students were next asked if monozygotic twins have one-half soul each, and a stark majority, 65 students, said "no." When asked if human clones (if one day possible) had souls, 48 students replied "yes" and only four replied "no." Nineteen students didn't know. The last question queried when the soul participates in the life of a human during development. Answers ranged from "before fertilization" to personal explanations, with no majority in any answer.

Formation of a Concept

Without a doubt, the definition of personhood is highly complex. New medical and genetic techniques only further complicate the issue of identifying personhood. Embryonic stem cell research, cloning, and sex changes are occurring today. Politics, government, and the workings of society convolute the definition even more. When Justice Harry Blackmun delivered the Supreme Court's opinion on personhood in *Roe v. Wade* in 1973, he presented that the Constitution does not define "person," and thus the unborn fetus is not a person under the 14th Amendment. Women's rights are closely linked to abortion issues, as well as health and privacy rights, and even human cloning (women would be needed as uterine hosts for clones). Which person engaged in any of these debates has more rights, or is correct or incorrect? Entangled with these decisions for each person are gender issues, social issues, and rights issues. The list goes on and on.

Who we are will define what we do. But do we define ourselves? Perhaps we do. The English philosopher John Locke once said, "Consider what person stands for; which, I think, is a thinking, intelligent being, that has reason and reflection." Considering at least what students have said in our small survey, Locke's opinion may very well be that of a minority today; recall that more than half of the surveyed students considered a clinically brain-dead individual to still exist as a person. Androids and robots in science fiction and the movies have often been portrayed as longing to be human. There is something about being a *person*, in addition to the vulnerable but dynamic organism that we call a human being, that is undeniably unique in this world—whether it is a scientific, philosophical, or spiritual phenomenon, or a result of a multitude of other possibilities, we cannot yet conclude. Whatever our origins, stage in evolutionary continuum, cultural values, or religious roots, we know of no single truth; what we do know is that it is all quite personal.

> *"It has been said that the modern animal rights movement is the first social reform movement initiated by philosophers."*

Animals Deserve to Be Recognized as Persons

Steven M. Wise

In the following viewpoint, Steven M. Wise traces the history of humankind's treatment of animal rights, from the ancient Greek philosophers to the twenty-first century US courts. Early Greeks held animals in high esteem, but the treatment of animals has steadily eroded over time. Animals have been compared to enslaved people, put on earth to serve the needs of their "superiors." Philosophers, noting that animals suffer as humans do, have led the movement to grant animals more rights. Judges have been slow to agree with such philosophies, but the battle for animal personhood continues. Steven M. Wise is founder and president of the Non-human Rights Project (NhRP). He has practiced animal protection law for 30 years throughout the United States.

"Animal Rights," by Steven M. Wise, Encyclopædia Britannica, Inc., August 18, 2016. Reprinted by permission.

As you read, consider the following questions:

1. Why did early classical philosophers consider animals sacred?
2. How have animal rights been compared to the rights of enslaved people?
3. How has the concept of animal personhood been taken up in recent court cases?

Animal rights [are] moral or legal entitlements attributed to nonhuman animals, usually because of the complexity of their cognitive, emotional, and social lives or their capacity to experience physical or emotional pain or pleasure. Historically, different views of the scope of animal rights have reflected philosophical and legal developments, scientific conceptions of animal and human nature, and religious and ethical conceptions of the proper relationship between animals and human beings.

Philosophical Background

The proper treatment of animals is a very old question in the West. Ancient Greek and Roman philosophers debated the place of animals in human morality. The Pythagoreans (6th–4th century BCE) and the Neoplatonists (3rd–6th century CE) urged respect for animals' interests, primarily because they believed in the transmigration of souls between human and animal bodies. In his biological writings, Aristotle (384–322 BCE) repeatedly suggested that animals lived for their own sake, but his claim in the *Politics* that nature made all animals for the sake of humans was unfortunately destined to become his most influential statement on the subject.

Aristotle, and later the Stoics, believed the world was populated by an infinity of beings arranged hierarchically according to their complexity and perfection, from the barely living to the merely sentient, the rational, and the wholly spiritual. In this Great Chain of Being, as it came to be known, all forms of life were represented as existing for the sake of those forms higher in the chain. Among corporeal beings, humans, by dint of their rationality, occupied the highest position. The Great Chain of Being became one of the most persistent and powerful, if utterly erroneous, ways of conceiving the universe, dominating scientific, philosophical, and religious thinking until the middle of the 19th century.

The Stoics, insisting on the irrationality of all nonhuman animals, regarded them as slaves and accordingly treated them as contemptible and beneath notice. Aggressively advocated by St. Augustine (354–430), these Stoic ideas became embedded in Christian theology. They were absorbed wholesale into Roman law—as reflected in the treatises and codifications of Gaius (fl. 130–180) and Justinian (483–565)—taken up by the legal glossators of Europe in the 11th century, and eventually pressed into English (and, much later, American) common law. Meanwhile, arguments that urged respect for the interests of animals nearly disappeared, and animal welfare remained a relative backwater of philosophical inquiry and legal regulation until the final decades of the 20th century.

Animals and the Law

In the 3rd or 4th century CE, the Roman jurist Hermogenianus wrote, "Hominum causa omne jus constitum" ("All law was established for men's sake"). Repeating the phrase, P.A. Fitzgerald's 1966 treatise *Salmond on Jurisprudence* declared, "The law is made for men and allows no fellowship or bonds of obligation between them and the lower animals." The most important consequence of this view is that animals have long been categorized as "legal things," not as "legal persons." Whereas legal persons have rights of their own, legal things do not. They exist in the law solely as the objects of the rights of legal persons—e.g., as things over which legal persons may exercise property rights. This status, however, often affords animals the indirect protection of laws intended to preserve social morality or the rights of animal owners, such as criminal anticruelty statutes or civil statutes that permit owners to obtain compensation for damages inflicted on their animals. Indeed, this sort of law presently defines the field of "animal law," which is much broader than animal rights because it encompasses all law that addresses the interests of nonhuman animals—or, more commonly, the interests of the people who own them.

A legal thing can become a legal person; this happened whenever human slaves were freed. The former legal thing then possesses his own legal rights and remedies. Parallels have frequently been drawn between the legal status of animals and that of human slaves. "The truly striking fact about slavery," the American historian David Brion Davis has written, is the

> antiquity and almost universal acceptance of the concept of the slave as a human being who is legally owned, used, sold, or otherwise disposed of as if he or she were a domestic animal. This parallel persisted in the similarity of naming slaves, branding them, and even pricing them according to their equivalent in cows, camels, pigs, and chickens.

The American jurist Roscoe Pound wrote that in ancient Rome a slave "was a thing, and as such, like animals could be the object of rights of property," and the British historian of Roman law Barry Nicholas has pointed out that in Rome "the slave was a thing… he himself had no rights: he was merely an object of rights, like an animal."

In the late 18th and early 19th centuries, humanitarian reformers in Britain and the United States campaigned on behalf of the weak and defenseless, protesting against child labour, debtor's prisons, abusive punishment in public schools, and, inevitably, the cruel treatment of animals. In 1800 the most renowned abolitionist of the period, William Wilberforce, supported a bill to abolish bull- and bearbaiting, which was defeated in the House of Commons. In 1809 Baron Erskine, former lord chancellor of England, who had long been troubled by cruelty to animals, introduced a bill to prohibit cruelty to all domestic animals. Erskine declared that the bill was intended to "consecrate, perhaps, in all nations, and in all ages, that just and eternal principle which binds the whole living world in one harmonious chain, under the dominion of enlightened man, the lord and governor of all." Although the bill passed the House of Lords, it failed in the House of Commons. Then, in 1821, a bill "to prevent cruel and improper treatment of Cattle" was introduced in the House of Commons, sponsored by Wilberforce and Thomas Fowell Buxton and championed by Irish member of Parliament Richard Martin. The version enacted in 1822, known as Martin's Act, made it a crime to treat a handful of domesticated animals—cattle, oxen, horses, and sheep—cruelly or to inflict unnecessary suffering upon them. However, it did not protect the general welfare of even these animals, much less give them legal rights, and the worst punishment available for any breach was a modest fine. Similar statutes were enacted in all the states of the United States, where there now exists a patchwork of anticruelty and animal-welfare laws. Most states today make at least some abuses of animals a felony. Laws such as the federal Animal Welfare Act (1966), for example, regulate what humans may do to animals in agriculture, biomedical research, entertainment, and other areas. But neither Martin's Act nor many subsequent animal-protection statutes altered the traditional legal status of animals as legal things.

This situation changed in 2008, when the Spanish national parliament adopted resolutions urging the government to grant orangutans, chimpanzees, and gorillas some statutory rights previously afforded only to humans. The resolutions also called for banning the use of apes in performances, harmful research, and trading as well as in other practices that involve profiting from the animals. Although zoos would still be allowed to hold apes, they would be required to provide them with "optimal" living conditions.

The Modern Animal Rights Movement

The fundamental principle of the modern animal rights movement is that many nonhuman animals have basic interests that deserve recognition, consideration, and protection. In the view of animal rights advocates, these basic interests give the animals that have them both moral and legal rights.

It has been said that the modern animal rights movement is the first social reform movement initiated by philosophers. The Australian philosopher Peter Singer and the American philosopher Tom Regan deserve special mention, not just because their work has been influential but because they represent two major currents of philosophical thought regarding the moral rights of animals. Singer, whose book *Animal Liberation* (1975) is considered one of the movement's foundational documents, argues that the interests of humans and the interests of animals should be given equal consideration. A utilitarian, Singer holds that actions are morally right to the extent that they maximize pleasure or minimize pain; the key consideration is whether an animal is sentient and can therefore suffer pain or experience pleasure. This point was emphasized by the founder of modern utilitarianism, Jeremy Bentham, who wrote of animals, "The question is not, Can they reason?, nor, Can they talk? but, Can they suffer?" Given that animals can suffer, Singer argues that humans have a moral obligation to minimize or avoid causing such suffering, just as they have an obligation to minimize or avoid causing the suffering of other humans. Regan, who is not a utilitarian, argues that at least some animals have basic moral rights because they possess the same advanced cognitive abilities that justify the attribution of basic moral rights to humans. By virtue of these abilities, these animals have not just instrumental but inherent value. In Regan's words, they are "the subject of a life."

Regan, Singer, and other philosophical proponents of animal rights have encountered resistance. Some religious authors argue that animals are not as deserving of moral consideration as humans are because only humans possess an immortal soul. Others claim, as did the Stoics, that because animals are irrational, humans have no duties toward them. Still others locate the morally relevant difference between humans and animals in the ability to talk, the possession of free will, or membership in a moral community (a community whose members are capable of acting morally or immorally). The problem with these counterarguments is that, with the exception of the theological argument—which cannot be demonstrated—none differentiates all humans from all animals.

While philosophers catalyzed the modern animal rights movement, they were soon joined by physicians, writers, scientists, academics, lawyers, theologians, psychologists, nurses, veterinarians, and other professionals, who worked within their own fields to promote animal rights. Many professional organizations were established to educate colleagues and the general public regarding the exploitation of animals.

At the beginning of the 21st century, lawsuits in the interests of nonhuman animals, sometimes with nonhuman animals named as plaintiffs, became common. Given the key positions that lawyers hold in the creation of public policy and the protection of rights, their increasing interest in animal rights and animal-protection issues was significant. Dozens of law schools in Europe, the United States, and elsewhere offered courses in animal law and animal rights; the Animal Legal Defense Fund had created an even greater number of law-student chapters in the United States; and at least three legal journals—*Animal Law, Journal of Animal Law,* and *Journal of Animal Law and Ethics*—had been established. Legal scholars were devising and evaluating theories by which nonhuman animals would possess basic legal rights, often for the same reasons as humans do and on the basis of the same legal principles and values. These arguments were powerfully assisted by increasingly sophisticated scientific investigations into the cognitive, emotional, and social capacities of animals and by advances in genetics, neuroscience, physiology, linguistics, psychology, evolution, and ethology, many of which have demonstrated that humans and animals share a broad range of behaviours, capacities, and genetic material.

Meanwhile, the increasingly systemic and brutal abuses of animals in modern society—by the billions on factory farms and by the tens of millions in biomedical-research laboratories—spawned thousands of animal rights groups. Some consisted of a mere handful of people interested in local, and more traditional, animal-protection issues, such as animal shelters that care for stray dogs and cats. Others became large national and international organizations, such as PETA (People for the Ethical Treatment of Animals) and the Humane Society of the United States, which in the early 21st century had millions of members and a multimillion-dollar annual budget. In all their manifestations, animal rights groups began to inundate legislatures with demands for regulation and reform.

Slaves, human and nonhuman, may be indirectly protected through laws intended to protect others. But they remain invisible to civil law, for they have no rights to protect directly until their legal personhood is recognized. This recognition can occur in a variety of ways. British slavery was abolished by judicial decision in the 18th century, and slavery in the British colonies was ended by statute early in the 19th century. By constitutional amendment, the United States ended slavery three decades later. Legal personhood for some animals may be obtained through any of these routes.

In 2013 the Nonhuman Rights Project (NhRP) filed petitions in three trial courts in the state of New York demanding that common law writs of habeas corpus be issued on behalf of four captive chimpanzees—Tommy, Kiko, Hercules, and Leo. The petitions implicitly asked that the courts recognize that chimpanzees are legal persons who possess the fundamental legal right to bodily liberty. After all three petitions were denied, the cases moved to the New York state appellate courts, where two of the petitions (on behalf of Tommy and Kiko) were rejected on differing grounds and the third (on behalf of Hercules and Leo) was thrown out for lack of the right to appeal. The NhRP then indicated its intention to appeal Tommy's and Kiko's cases to New York's highest court, the Court of Appeals, and to refile Hercules and Leo's petition in another jurisdiction. Meanwhile, the organization prepared to file additional lawsuits on behalf of other chimpanzees and elephants.

*"We cannot morally justify exploiting
animals for experiments any more
than experiments on mental patients
or babies can be justified."*

Animals Have a Right to Be Free of Human Use and Exploitation

Doris Lin

In the following viewpoint, Doris Lin argues that animals should not be used for human needs. Lin does not suggest that animals have the same rights as humans but that they should be treated as sentient beings that suffer. Humans use animals for everything from food to medical experimentation. Lin believes that virtually none of these reasons is valid. The author distinguishes between the concept of "animal welfare" and "animal rights" and favors the latter over the former. She rejects speciesism, the concept that humans are superior to animals and therefore may exploit the lower species. Doris Lin is an animal rights attorney and the director of legal affairs for the Animal Protection League of New Jersey.

"What Are Animal Rights? Do Animal Rights Activists Want Animals to Have the Same Rights as People?" by Doris Lin, Dotdash Publishing Family, January 8, 2018. Reprinted by permission.

As you read, consider the following questions:

1. According to the author, what animal products do humans not need?
2. What are the common justifications for the use of animals?
3. According to the author, what distinguishes animal rights from animal welfare?

A nimal rights are the belief that animals have a right to be free of human use and exploitation, but there is a great deal of confusion about what that means. Animal rights are not about putting animals above humans or giving animals the same rights as humans. Also, animal rights are very different from animal welfare.

To most animal rights activists, animal rights are grounded in a rejection of speciesism and the knowledge that animals have sentience (the ability to suffer).

Freedom from Human Use and Exploitation

Humans use and exploit animals in myriad ways, including meat, milk, eggs, animal experimentation, fur, hunting, and circuses.

With the possible exception of animal experimentation, all of these uses of animals are frivolous. People don't need meat, eggs, milk, fur, hunting or circuses. The American Dietetic Association recognizes that people can be perfectly healthy as vegans.

Regarding animal experimentation, most would agree that testing of cosmetics and household products is unnecessary. A new furniture polish or lipstick seems a frivolous reason to blind, maim, and kill hundreds or thousands of rabbits.

Many would also say that scientific experimentation on animals for the sake of science, with no immediate, obvious application to human health, is unnecessary because the suffering of the animals outweighs the satisfaction of human curiosity. This leaves only medical experiments. While animal experimentation may lead to human medical advancements, we cannot morally justify exploiting animals for experiments any more than experiments on mental patients or babies can be justified.

Justifications for Animal Exploitation

The most common justifications for animal use are:

- Animals are not intelligent (cannot think/reason).
- Animals are not as important as people.
- Animals have no duties.
- God put animals here for us to use.

Rights cannot be determined by the ability to think, or we'd have to give intelligence tests to determine which humans deserve rights. This would mean that babies, the mentally disabled and the mentally ill would have no rights.

Importance is not a good criterion for rights holding because importance is highly subjective and individuals have their own interests that make each individual important to him/herself. One person may find that their own pets are more important to them than a stranger on the other side of the world, but that doesn't give them the right to kill and eat that stranger.

The President of United States might be more important than most people, but that doesn't give the president the right to kill people and mount their heads on the wall as trophies. One could also argue that a single blue whale is more important than any single human being because the species is endangered and every individual is needed to help the population recover.

Duties are also not good criteria for rights holding because individuals who are incapable of recognizing or performing duties, such as babies or people with profound disabilities, still have a right not to be eaten or experimented on. Furthermore, animals are routinely killed for failing to follow human rules (e.g., the mouse who is killed in a mousetrap), so even if they have no duties, we punish them for failing to abide by our expectations.

Religious beliefs are also an inappropriate determination of rights holding because religious beliefs are highly subjective and personal. Even within a religion, people will disagree about what God dictates. We shouldn't impose our religious beliefs on others, and using religion to justify animal exploitation imposes our religion on the animals. And keep in mind that the Bible was once used to justify the enslavement of Africans and African Americans in the United States, demonstrating how people often use religion as an excuse to further their personal beliefs.

Because there will always be some humans who don't fit the criteria used to justify animal exploitation, the only true distinction between humans and non-human animals are species, which is an arbitrary line to draw between which individuals do and don't have rights. There is no magical dividing line between humans and non-human animals.

The Same Rights as Humans?

There is a common misconception that animal rights activists want non-human animals to have the same rights as people. No one wants cats to have the right to vote, or for dogs to have the right to bear arms. The issue is not whether animals should have the same rights as people, but whether we have a right to use and exploit them for our purposes, however frivolous they might be.

Animal Rights v. Animal Welfare

Animal rights are distinguishable from animal welfare. In general, the term "animal rights" is the belief that humans do not have a right to use animals for our own purposes. "Animal welfare" is the belief that humans do have a right to use animals as long as the animals are treated humanely. The animal rights position on factory farming would be that we do not have a right to slaughter animals for food no matter how well the animals are treated while they are alive, while the animal welfare position might want to see certain cruel practices eliminated.

"Animal welfare" describes a broad spectrum of views, while animal rights are more absolute. For example, some animal welfare

A MUDDLED ALTERNATIVE TO REAL PROTECTION

The push to create animal personhood within the law only goes so far. It happily includes primates, domestic and companion animals, elephants, dolphins, and the like. But it would enhance the legal status only of those animals that stand within the light of the human campfire, animals on whom it's easy to project human qualities like "intelligence," animals that have an obvious economic utility or that readily appear to be capable of suffering cruelty. It stops well short, to put it mildly, of insisting on something far more fundamental: that all species have an equal and equivalent right to their own existence. Even to call this a "right" is to fall into a familiar legalistic and linguistic trap. We don't have a word—much less a concept in law—to suggest that the existence of any species is its own sufficient justification, a justification that applies to every species, including us, whose justification is in no way superior to that of other species. In the Western tradition, God was the guarantor of the equivalence of all species. God was also, of course, the grantor to humans of dominion over all species.

The important question is this: How do we restrain humanity enough to allow the continuing coexistence of other species? I wish I believed that a fiction like the legal personhood of animals could really help do it. But I don't. To ask humans to deny themselves for the benefit of any other species, especially those that lie outside our immediate awareness, seems to be asking what is nearly impossible. We're blinded by our self-regard, or perhaps we're just inherently blind. It's profoundly difficult to feel our kinship with all other species, whether kinship is expressed as an overwhelming overlap of DNA or the shared occupancy of this earth or any other way you like. We have to imagine it, construct it in our minds, actively engage the thought. And even then, it remains a thought, and thought—compared with hunger and habit—is barely able to influence our actions.

"Animal 'Personhood': Muddled Alternative to Real Protection," by Verlyn Klinkenborg, Yale Environment 360, January 30, 2014.

advocates might want a ban on fur, while others might believe that fur is morally acceptable if the animals are killed "humanely" and do not suffer for too long in a trap. "Animal welfare" may also be used to describe the speciesist view that certain animals (e.g. dogs, cats, horses) are more deserving of protection than others (e.g. fish, chickens, cows).

> "*The emerging international rights-of-nature movement aims to address the way western legal systems treat nature as property, making the living world invisible to the law.*"

Nature Deserves Legal Rights

Jane Gleeson-White

In the following viewpoint, Jane Gleeson-White addresses the notion of personhood for nature, including rivers, mountains, and forests. The author presents current cases from Ecuador, New Zealand, and Australia. Giving nature legal rights not only protects the natural world, she maintains, but coincides with the belief system of the Aboriginal peoples who first inhabited Australia. Jane Gleeson-White is author of four books. Her essays and articles on literature, economics, and sustainability have been published widely.

As you read, consider the following questions:

1. What benefits are there to giving nature legal rights?
2. How does the rights-for-nature philosophy differ from traditional approaches to preserving the natural world?
3. How does the rights-for-nature movement coincide with the beliefs of Aboriginal peoples in Australia?

On 20 March a community rally on the Margaret river south of Perth called for the river to be recognised as a legal entity with the local council as its custodian. Under the banner "Is it time to give our river rights?," more than 100 people discussed ways of protecting the river, prompted by plans for a mountain-bike and walking track along the foreshore. A river advocate, Ray Swarts, says a rights-of-nature approach has majority support in the council.

The emerging international rights-of-nature movement aims to address the way western legal systems treat nature as property, making the living world invisible to the law. It uses western legal constructs, such as personhood and rights-based approaches, to shift the status of nature from property to a subject in law in an effort to protect the natural world.

This new approach to environmental law was introduced in the US by the Community Environmental Legal Defense Fund, whose first success came in 2006 when it helped to defend a Pennsylvania community's right to reject sludge being dumped in their borough.

In just over a decade the rights-of-nature movement has grown from one law adopted in a small community in the US to a movement which has seen countries enact laws, even constitutional protections, recognising the rights of nature, says the fund's co-founder, Margi Margil.

In 2008 Ecuador became the first country to enshrine the rights of nature in its constitution. Margil helped draft the legislation and says that during the process: "Indigenous members of Ecuador's constitutional assembly told us that codifying the rights of nature would expand their collective rights as Indigenous peoples."

New Zealand granted legal personhood to the TeUruwera forest in 2014, and to the Whanganui river and Mount Taranaki in 2017. An Indian court granted legal personhood to the Ganges and Yamuna rivers in 2017, citing the Whanganui Act, and soon after Colombia awarded rights to the Atrato river.

In a significant shift, in an August 2017 report on Australia's national environmental governance system, the Australian panel of experts on environmental law recommended exploring legal frameworks that shift the focus of law from human subjects to a "rights of nature" approach.

Traditional owners along the Kimberley's Fitzroy river are also looking at ways to create legal personhood for their river. Their 2016 Fitzroy river declaration recognises the river as a living ancestral being with a right to life, and includes traditional owners' obligation to protect the river for current and future generations. A traditional custodian and scientist, Dr. Anne Poelina, says it's "the first time in Australia that both first law and the inherent rights of nature have been explicitly recognised in a negotiated instrument." This month community members urged the new Labor state government to uphold their pre-election commitment to the declaration.

Rights for nature were first proposed by Christopher Stone in his 1972 article "Should trees have standing?" and were famously endorsed by Justice William O. Douglas's dissenting judgment in *Sierra Club v Morton*, in which he argued that trees should be granted personhood and have the ability to sue for their own protection. Stone argued that leaving behind the enlightenment view of nature as a collection of "useful senseless objects" would not only help to solve the planet's material problems but would encourage a heightened awareness of nature.

"Any system that puts no value on the life around us is wrong, it's as simple as that," says Dr. Michelle Maloney, who co-founded the Australian Earth Laws Alliance in 2012 to promote rights-of-nature law in Australia. She says rights of nature is inspired and led by Indigenous traditions of Earth-centred law and culture, but it's also "white fellas talking back to the white system."

"It's looking back to the western legal governance system and going, 'What kind of culture develops the systems we have now that created such devastation? Can rights of nature be a bridge into a different, Earth-centred way of being?'"

It was Maloney who introduced rights-of-nature thinking to the Margaret river. She says the alliance's recommendation that

Human-Style Rights Should Not Be Applied to Nature

How can the law account for the value of complex, nonhuman entities such as rivers, lakes, forests and ecosystems? At a time of runaway climate change, when the Earth's biosphere is on the brink of collapse and species extinctions are accelerating, this has become a vital question.

Some theorists argue that there's a clear historical precedent for what we should do, arising from the struggle for universal human rights. The law and discourse of human rights, commonly traced back to the Enlightenment, has held sway over the sections of the Western public for decades, if not centuries. Perhaps we should take the idea of "the human" as a rights-bearer and extend it to the complex, nonhuman systems that we wish to protect, that we know are deserving of care and concern.

Tempting as it is, this move must be resisted. For one thing, human rights have proven to be exclusionary—even within our own species. Its emergence as a set of legal and moral norms betrays the fact that the white, European, male property-owner is the paradigm case of "the human": others, historically, have had to fight even to be seen as fully capable of bearing rights. International treaties have been required to address the rights of women, children, workers, LGBT people, indigenous communities and others, *precisely* because such "minorities" were marginalised by the abstract idea of "the human" of the Universal Declaration of Human Rights. Critics have also suggested that human rights norms are a Trojan horse for neo-imperialism, providing ideological cover for dubious "humanitarian" interventions and capitalist plundering. In theory, human rights are for all humans, but it turns out that some people are more human than others.

Yet maybe there's something to be salvaged from rights discourse all the same—if we can find a way to deploy the idea of "rights" while decentring "the human." Perhaps we can find ways of understanding ourselves as entangled partners, and sometimes co-sufferers, with nonhuman animals, beings and systems in a "more-than-human world," as the gender scholar Astrida Neimanis at the University of Sydney put it in an article in 2014.

"It's Wrongheaded to Protect Nature with Human-Style Rights," by Anna Grear, Aeon Media Group Ltd, March 19, 2019.

rights of nature be explored in Australia is "huge for the legal community here." She's now working with communities along the Great Barrier Reef and this month addressed a gathering in Katoomba about rights of nature for the Blue Mountains.

Maloney says it's powerful "because it can capture your imagination and encourage you to think differently. To all non-lawyers, it seems logical." Ray Swarts concurs: "I think rights-of-nature law helps us personalise and reframe our relationship with nature. It puts it in a different context and starts to tell a story."

Stories were vital in developing Australia's first legislation with a rights-of-nature component, the Yarra River Protection (Wilip-gin Birrarungmurron) Act 2017. The act affirms the river's intrinsic and human values, and recognises the river and lands as a living and integrated system.

In doing so it acknowledges the wisdom of its traditional owners, the Wurundjeri people, who introduced the bill into the Victorian parliament with the planning minister, Richard Wynne, last June. Wynne said the legislation was part of a broader movement in government to recognise Aboriginal rights to land.

In her address to the parliament, the Wurundjeri elder Alice Kolasa said: "The state now recognises something that we, as the First People have always known, that the Birrarung is one integrated living entity." She said the journey to this structural inclusion began from the moment of first contact.

The act recognises "the intrinsic connection of the traditional owners to the Yarra river and its country" and their role "as the custodians of the land and waterway which they call Birrarung." It includes their Woi-wurrung language, making it the first legislation in Victoria to use the language of traditional owners. Its title contains the Woi-wurrung for "Keep the Birrarung alive" and its preamble includes a statement in Woi-wurrung about the Birrarung's significance.

Conceiving the Yarra river and its lands as a single system is critical for its ecological health. In 2004 the Yarra Riverkeeper Association was formed to tell the river's story and monitor its health. Before the 2014 state election it proposed a policy to protect the Yarra with consistent planning laws along the river. The then opposition Labor party committed to the plan and won the election.

A Yarra Riverkeeper, Andrew Kelly, worked with a lawyer, Bruce Lindsay, from Environmental Justice Australia, to keep Labor to its promise and help develop the Yarra river protection act, with extensive community consultation. Lindsay saw it as a good opportunity for law reform, especially concerning water.

Kelly says the plan surfed a wave of enthusiasm: "It was a really fortunate conjunction of the stars that allowed this to happen." The long-term Yarra strategic plan was critical for Kelly and Lindsay: "We didn't want to plan for five years. We wanted to plan for 50 years. That's what you've got to start thinking about when you're dealing with ecological units, landscapes."

Some people think the act is about the water, Kelly says. "But it's really more about the banks. It's as much about the birds as it is about the fish. It's about connecting the length of the waterway and the riverine corridor."

Lindsay hopes the act's powerful bicultural element will lead to a bicultural understanding of the river. A water lawyer, Erin O'Donnell, also stresses its importance as a piece of bilingual legislation. She emphasises the symbolic value of creating an inclusive Birrarung council that has the power to genuinely provide a voice for the Yarra river. "If through the Birrarung council First Nations and all Yarra river stakeholders can come together, this could be a powerful model for the rest of Australia … It can be used as a genuine move towards reconciliation. It's a pathway to legitimacy for holistic views of the river and acknowledgment of First Nations."

From the Fitzroy river, Poelina says she's inspired by the Yarra river protection act and fully endorses "the Yarra river's right to life as a legal precedent for new laws to protect our Australian rivers which are the arteries of our nation. As my elders constantly remind me: no river, no people, no life!"

> "The Global Slavery Index
> 2018 estimates that there were
> 40.3 million people trapped in
> modern slavery on any given day
> in 2016. Ten million of them are
> considered to be children and 71% of
> everyone trapped in modern slavery
> is a woman or girl."

Human Trafficking Denies Personhood to Individuals

The Justice and Peace Office of the Catholic Archdiocese of Sydney

In the following viewpoint, the Justice and Peace Office of the Catholic Archdiocese of Sydney argues that, although slavery is outlawed in every country on Earth, the number of enslaved people is likely larger than when slavery was legal. While countries such as Australia have enacted legislation against such trade, the practical effect of these laws remains to be seen. Fighting the greed and corruption that causes human trafficking is a difficult undertaking. Enormous amounts of money are at stake, and this emboldens traffickers. Victims suffer trauma and loss, and the prospect of multigenerational degradation. The Justice and Peace Office of the Catholic Archdiocese of Sydney promotes justice, peace, ecology, and development through projects and activities based on the social teachings of the Catholic Church.

As you read, consider the following questions:

1. How is modern slavery defined?
2. Why has there been increased trade in human slaves lately?
3. How do consumers unwittingly contribute to human trafficking?

M odern slavery is a broad term that encompasses a number of unethical practices such as slavery or forced labour (including child labour), debt bondage, slavery-like practices, servitude, deceptive recruiting, forced marriage, prostitution, organ trafficking and human trafficking. Modern slavery is different to historical forms of slavery, especially what is referred to as "chattel slavery," in which it was legal in many jurisdictions for one human being to own another human being outright, to buy, sell or inherit that human being, to exploit him or her or deprive that person of life, without any repercussions for the person who harmed them. Chattel slavery and the slave trade are now illegal in every country in the world and under international law (Article 4 of the Universal Declaration of Human Rights). However, estimates say there are more people trapped in conditions of modern slavery today than there were slaves, even when slavery was legal.

What Is Human Trafficking?

Trafficking in humans is the equivalent of the modern day slave-trade. The UN defines "Trafficking in persons" as the "recruitment, transportation, transfer, harbouring or receipt of persons, by means of the threat or use of force or other forms of coercion, of abduction, of fraud, of deception, of the abuse of power or of a position of vulnerability or of the giving or receiving of payments or benefits to achieve the consent of a person having control over another person, for the purpose of exploitation" (Article 3(a) of the Protocol to Prevent, Suppress and Punish Trafficking in Persons Especially Women and Children, supplementing the

United Nations Convention against Transnational Organized Crime). Exploitation includes prostitution or other forms of sexual exploitation, forced labour or services, slavery or practices similar to slavery, servitude or the removal of organs. Trafficking can occur within one's own country or across international borders. Almost all the people who are trafficked end up in situations of modern slavery.

What Is the Situation in New South Wales?

In 2018, the New South Wales Parliament also passed the Modern Slavery Act 2018 (NSW). It requires companies that have revenue over $50 million (AUD) a year to report on the risks of modern slavery in their supply chains and there are strong fines for not complying with this requirement. The NSW Act also provides for an Anti-Slavery Commissioner with wide ranging powers to advocate for and promote action to combat modern slavery. However, the NSW Act has not yet entered force and is currently under Parliamentary review with the Committee expected to table its report in late March 2020.

What Is the Situation in Australia?

Slavery, human trafficking and related practices such as servitude, forced labour, deceptive recruiting, trafficking in persons, debt bondage and organ trafficking are illegal in Australia under the Divisions 270 and 271 of the Criminal Code (found in the Schedule to the Criminal Code Act 1995). Despite it being illegal, the Global Slavery Index estimates say that there are approximately 15,000 people living under conditions of modern slavery in Australia in 2018 and because of the clandestine nature of the activity, the real numbers are probably much higher. Despite the illegal nature of slavery, convictions are rare. Between 2004-2018 the Commonwealth Director of Public Prosecutions only prosecuted 19 people for slavery related offences.

In 2018 the Federal Government also passed the Modern Slavery Act 2018 which requires businesses which have a consolidated revenue over $100 million (AUD) a year to compile a Modern Slavery Statement on the risk of modern slavery in their supply chains and what they are doing to remedy it. The statements need to be approved by the board of directors or signed by a director. The Australian Government is also required to publish a modern slavery statement on its public procurement. The Australian Government will provide for these statements to be made publicly available online. It is hoped that the public register of Modern Slavery Statements will allow everyone to see the extent of modern slavery in companies' supply chains and put public pressure on them to eliminate slavery from their processes. What concrete effect the Modern Slavery Statements will have on eliminating slavery will need to be seen.

What Is the Situation Globally?

The Global Slavery Index 2018 estimates that there were 40.3 million people trapped in modern slavery on any given day in 2016. Ten million of them are considered to be children and 71% of everyone trapped in modern slavery is a woman or girl. They estimate that 24.9 million people are trapped in forced labour and 15.4 million people are trapped in forced marriages. The sad reality is that as with many clandestine activities, the true numbers are probably much higher. Modern slavery and human trafficking are incredibly lucrative transnational criminal industries. In 2014, the International Labor Organisation estimated that forced labour generated $150 billion US Dollars in revenue for the perpetrators.

Modern Slavery and the Sustainable Development Goals

The international community has recognised the prevalence of modern slavery and its dangers and has therefore included Target 8.7 as one of the Sustainable Development Goals (SDG). Pope Francis was a key instigator in getting the goal of eradicating modern slavery included in the SDGs.

Target 8.7: Take immediate and effective measures to eradicate forced labour, end modern slavery and human trafficking and secure the prohibition and elimination of the worst forms of child labour, including recruitment and use of child soldiers, and by 2025 end child labour in all its forms

To implement Target 8.7, Alliance 8.7 has formed. Alliance 8.7 is a global partnership fostering multi-stakeholder collaboration to support governments in achieving Target 8.7 by 2030. Alliance 8.7 is tasked with promoting accelerated action to eradicate forced labour, modern slavery, human trafficking and child labour; research, data collection and knowledge sharing on prevalence and "what works"; and driving innovation and leveraging resources. There are a number or key groups that are working to combat modern slavery both in Australia and around the world.

Why Are They Such Big Problems Right Now?

Human trafficking and modern slavery have become a more serious problem in recent years because of governments and non-governmental organisations clamping down on the illegal sales of arms and drugs. Traffickers have discovered that instead of selling arms and drugs once, human beings can be sold over and over again, making them more profit.

These unethical practices enable people to be controlled, exploited and deprived of their innate dignity and freedom and are complex and entrenched problems that degrade our human family in a multitude of ways. While the Catholic Church (particularly religious congregations) has long been working to end trafficking and slavery and alleviate the suffering caused by such exploitation, Pope Francis is renewing and reinvigorating the Church's efforts. He has raised his voice against the growing "throw-away" culture giving rise to slavery and trafficking.

Today, as in the past, slavery is rooted in a notion of the human person which allows him or her to be treated as an object. Whenever sin corrupts the human heart and distances us from our Creator and our neighbours, the latter are no longer regarded as beings of equal dignity, as brothers or sisters sharing a common humanity, but rather as objects. Whether by coercion or deception, or by physical or psychological duress, human persons created in the image and likeness of God are deprived of their freedom, sold and reduced to being the property of others. They are treated as means to an end.

—Pope Francis, World Day of Peace Message 2015.

The innate dignity of each and every person and our shared equality as brothers and sisters in Christ are principles we can easily recognize as Catholics. Yet, when we participate in a culture or economy that makes people into objects or commodities to be used and thrown away, we are allowing people's innate dignity to be dismissed in favour of a monetary value. This tendency is compounded by society's preoccupation with money, financial gain and profit maximisation. The downside to this skewed culture is the consequent poverty, underdevelopment and exclusion that is prevalent globally. The desperate situation of people in extreme poverty, particularly where they may be lacking in education, makes them vulnerable to exploitation. Corrupt people facilitate and condone the exploitation of others and deception and violence (or the threat of violence) enforces compliance with those who exploit.

Various forms of exploitation or subjugation are of concern. Countries may fail to comply with international norms or standards regarding the treatment of labour in industries such as agriculture, mining or manufacture or otherwise poorly protect workers in practice. For example, relevant laws may exist but they may not be effectively enforced. Migrants may be inhumanely detained or abused or migrant workers (as distinct from citizens of a country) may live or work in degrading conditions. Prostitution, sex-slavery and forced marriage is also of grave concern. People may be forced into other illegal activities, such as: the sale of organs; recruitment as soldiers or otherwise used for the purposes of militia; thieving or begging; the sale of children; production, distribution or sale of illegal items. In addition, such exploitation can take place as a result of a process of trafficking victims. Traffickers may recruit or procure, harbour or transport people, either forcing, coercing or defrauding them so they travel to a different location where they are exploited once they arrive at their destination.

Trauma and loss are likely suffered as a result of such exploitation and this suffering may deleteriously impact victims long after the experience of slavery or trafficking has ceased. It may also impact the lives of their families and, particularly their children, contributing to a tragic intergenerational spiral of degradation.

How Does Human Trafficking or Modern Slavery Affect Me?

Even for those of us who are not directly involved in trafficking in persons or exploiting people under conditions of modern slavery, we may still be contributing to trafficking or modern slavery through the goods and services we purchase.

Despite popular perception, the most common form of modern slavery is forced labour, and not forced prostitution or sexual exploitation. Many of the items that can be purchased for extremely low costs such as clothes, shoes, tea, coffee and chocolate may well be produced by people who are trafficked and then forced to work in exploitative situations. In terms of services, beauty salons, restaurants and cafes, carwashes, fruit-picking and construction are some of the most common industries tainted by modern slavery. The vast majority of people who appear in pornographic videos are people who have been trafficked. To try to eliminate forced labour and undignified working conditions, we all need to be more careful about investigating the supply chain of the goods and services we purchase. Both the Vatican and the Catholic Archdiocese of Sydney have committed to the formidable task, as far as possible, to eliminate modern slavery from their supply chain of purchases.

> It is good for people to realize that purchasing is always a moral — and not simply economic — act. Hence the consumer has a specific social responsibility, which goes hand-in-hand with the social responsibility of the enterprise. Consumers should

be continually educated regarding their daily role, which can be exercised with respect for moral principles without diminishing the intrinsic economic rationality of the act of purchasing.

—Pope Benedict XVI, Caritas in Veritate, 66.

Our faith requires us to intervene, to take steps in favour of those who are currently exploited and to prevent others from entering slavery or being trafficked.

We ought to recognize that we are facing a global phenomenon which exceeds the competence of any one community or country. In order to eliminate it, we need a mobilization comparable in size to that of the phenomenon itself. For this reason I urgently appeal to all men and women of good will … not to become accomplices to this evil, not to turn away from the sufferings of our brothers and sisters, our fellow human beings, who are deprived of their freedom and dignity.

The globalization of indifference, which today burdens the lives of so many of our brothers and sisters, requires all of us to forge a new worldwide solidarity and fraternity capable of giving them new hope and helping them to advance with courage amid the problems of our time and the new horizons which they disclose and which God places in our hands.

—Pope Francis, World Peace Day Message 2015.

Periodical and Internet Sources Bibliography

The following articles have been selected to supplement the diverse views presented in this chapter.

Advocate Magazine, "When Animal 'Legal Personhood' Gets Personal," Summer 2014. https://law.lclark.edu/live/news/26010 -when-animal-legal-personhood-gets-personal

Associated Press, "Orangutan Who Was Granted 'Personhood' Celebrates 34th Birthday," *New York Daily News*, February 17, 2020. https://nypost.com/2020/02/17/orangutan-who-was -granted-personhood-celebrates-34th-birthday/

Tom L. Beauchamp, "The Failure of Theories of Personhood," *Kennedy Institute of Ethics Journal* 9.4 (1999) 309–324. http:// www.sci.brooklyn.cuny.edu/~schopra/Persons/beauchamp.html

Jennifer Bjorhus, "Minnesota Tribe Asks: Can Wild Rice Have Its Own Legal Rights?" *Star Tribune*, February 9, 2019. http://www .startribune.com/minnesota-tribe-asks-can-wild-rice-have-its -own-legal-rights/505618712/

Jason Daley, "Toledo, Ohio, Just Granted Lake Erie the Same Legal Rights as People," *Smithsonian Magazine*, March 1, 2019. https:// www.smithsonianmag.com/smart-/toledo-ohio-just-granted -lake-erie-same-legal-rights-people-180971603/

Tatiana Freiin von Rheinbaben, "The Non-Human Rights Project: Conferring Personhood to Non-Human Animals," McCoy Family Center for Ethics in Society, April 12, 2017. https:// ethicsinsociety.stanford.edu/research-outreach/buzz-blog/non -human-rights-project-conferring-personhood-non-human -animals

Gwendolyn J. Gordon, "Environmental Personhood," *Columbia Journal of Environmental Law* 43:1. https://faculty.wharton .upenn.edu/wp-content/uploads/2019/08/Gordon -Environmental-Personhood.pdf

Daniel McGraw, "Fighting Pollution: Toledo Residents Want Personhood Status for Lake Erie," *Guardian*, February 19, 2019. https://www.theguardian.com/us-news/2019/feb/19/lake-erie -pollution-personhood-status-toledo

Erin O'Donnell and Julia Talbot-Jones, "Three Rivers Are Now Legally People—but That's Just the Start of Looking After Them," The Conversation, March 23, 2017. https://theconversation.com /three-rivers-are-now-legally-people-but-thats-just-the-start-of -looking-after-them-74983

Mark Peters, "Why Personhood Is Powerful," *Boston Globe*, November 20, 2011. https://www.bostonglobe.com/ ideas/2011/11/20/why-personhood-powerful /VIAIpr5qXw8X5vOqs74y4H/story.html

Ed Quillen, "Personhood and Death," *Denver Post*, May 15, 2008. https://www.denverpost.com/2008/05/15/personhood-and -death/

University of Missouri School of Medicine, "Concept of Personhood," https://medicine.missouri.edu/centers-institutes-labs /health-ethics/faq/personhood

OPPOSING
VIEWPOINTS®
SERIES

CHAPTER 2

How Can Corporations Be Persons?

Chapter Preface

Two words, "Citizens United," validated the concept of corporate personhood in the United States and reverberated around the world. The US Supreme Court Case *Citizens United v. Federal Elections Commission* revolved around campaign finance laws, which had been tightened in previous years in an attempt to limit corruption in the American political system.

Citizens United is a conservative nonprofit organization that attempted to broadcast a film critical of Democratic presidential candidate Hillary Clinton just prior to the 2008 Democratic primary elections. Doing so would have violated the 2002 Bipartisan Campaign Reform Act, which prevented a labor union or corporation from making an "electioneering communication" within 30 days of a primary or 60 days of an election, or making any expenditure supporting or rejecting a candidate at any time.

The case went through the lower courts before, in a high profile ruling in 2010, the Supreme Court decided 5-4 that corporations were granted First Amendment rights. The decision meant that corporate political spending was protected speech under the First Amendment.

The practical meaning of this decision allowed for a deluge of monetary contributions to flood the US political system. It led to the rise of what is now known as the Super PAC, any group of like-minded citizens who join together to support or oppose a candidate or cause, raise money, and promote their interests through advertising or other means.

Super PACs are not bound by contribution limits and are able to accept donations from corporations and unions. They have this freedom because they operate independently of candidates and parties and are not allowed to coordinate their spending with these entities. Nevertheless, it does not take a particularly creative mind to see how Super PACs could abuse the system and get around these restrictions. Dark money contributions, for example, where the donor is unknown, have exploded in the post–*Citizens United* era. Such donors can now spend vast sums to influence US elections. Experts estimate that in 2020, well over a billion dollars in dark money flooded the US political system in an attempt to influence the presidential election.

But the decision did not grant full personhood to these groups. Corporations or labor unions could no more cast an election ballot than robots or rivers could. Nevertheless, these groups are now able to exert outsized influence on the political scene.

As with any hotly contested issue, debate around *Citizens United* has continued to rage since the Supreme Court ruling. Seeking a way around the Supreme Court decision, some groups have called for a constitutional amendment to ban dark money and other campaign finance loopholes. A group called American Promise has proposed an amendment to do just this. In justifying its proposal, American Promise makes this statement:

> "Corporate Personhood" is an umbrella term that refers to the many ways we treat corporations as people under the law. Sometimes this is helpful for how laws are applied—such as when the Clean Water Act prohibiting the dumping of waste materials into waterways is applied to corporations as well as individuals. Other times, however, when this concept is expanded to grant constitutional rights originally meant for people, it can have anti-democratic and socially destructive consequences.[1]

It is doubtful that groups such as American Promise can deliver on their goal to reinstate stricter campaign finance laws. The hurdles for creating a new amendment are so high that passage of such a law in a highly divided political landscape would be a herculean task. Moreover, for every progressive group trying to restore order to the wild west of current campaign finance laws, there are conservative groups that are just as dogged in their determination to maintain—or even expand—personhood status for corporations.

Endnotes

1. Susie Fagan, "5 Reasons We Need an Amendment to Say Corporations Aren't People," American Promise, April 10, 2019. https://americanpromise.net /blog/2019/04/10/5-reasons-we-need-an-amendment-to-say-corporations -arent-people

> *"If ordinary people are incipient business owners, then the reverse is also true: businesses are treated as people. This view, which dates back to nineteenth-century jurisprudence and the doctrine of 'corporate personhood,' has only accelerated in recent years."*

The History of Corporate Personhood Is Long

Lawrence B. Glickman

In the following viewpoint Lawrence B. Glickman debunks the notion that corporate involvement in American politics is a new development. He provides a history of business leaders' involvement in the political process, citing Calvin Coolidge's famous statement that the business of America is business. The late twentieth century produced arguments on both sides of the political spectrum, as muckraker Ralph Nader attacked the corporate world's profits-at-all-cost mentality, while economist Milton Friedman defended the corporate profit motive. Lawrence B. Glickman is the Stephen and Evalyn Milman Professor of American Studies in the Department of History at Cornell University. He is the author or editor of five books, including Free Enterprise: An American History *(2019).*

"Business as Usual: The Long History of Corporate Personhood," by Lawrence B. Glickman, *Boston Review* and its authors, August 23, 2017. Reprinted by permission.

As you read, consider the following questions:

1. How does the author defend his argument that corporate involvement in politics is not new?
2. What is Lewis Powell's argument regarding business and politics and how was it influential?
3. How does Glickman find fault with the idea, expressed by David Gelles and Howard Shultz, suggesting that corporate ethical decisions are not always business based?

The mass defection of CEOs of some of the nation's most powerful corporations from President Trump's now-defunct Manufacturing Jobs Initiative and his Strategy and Policy Forum has led to a spate of commentary about the turn of business leaders to politics, much of it suggesting that this is a new phenomenon. "This is a remarkable moment in history," observes Lou Dobbs, the business journalist turned right-wing political commentator. Dobbs is quoted in a recent celebratory *New York Times* article by David Gelles on corporate executives. Also quoted in the article is Darren Walker, president of the Ford Foundation, who states, "In this maelstrom, the most clarifying voice has been the voice of business."

There is an emerging mythology around the involvement of business elites in politics—recent commentary marks it as a new phase of corporate activism, a radical break from the past. "Companies got political only under duress," Gelles claims. These commentaries suggest that businesses have been forced against their will into the political fray. "Companies are naturally designed to be moneymaking enterprises," writes Gelles. The assumption here is not only that businesses have been brought unwillingly into the political arena but that the innate purpose of business—moneymaking—is outside of the realm of politics. The reality is that business "got political" a long time ago; indeed, it has consistently been one of the most powerful forces in American political life. How did this story come to be obscured?

One answer is that both business leaders and pundits have emphasized business's role in the culture wars while minimizing its role in the class war. Politics is about "taking a stand or adopting a cause," as Marc Benioff, the CEO of Salesforce, told Gelles, "cause" being understood here not as capital gains tax rates, but as engaging in social issues. This perspective limits the boundaries of politics to "speaking out" on controversial social issues. And it ignores the "stands" that corporate leaders take on economic issues—regulation and anti-trust, for example. In this telling, their positions are less acts of politics than of doing what comes naturally and spontaneously for people oriented toward profit-making as their *raison d'être*.

There are at least two other reasons for the obfuscation of corporate politics. One is that business advocates since the New Deal have claimed that their political forays are purely defensive. Another is that commentators have fenced economics off from politics, so that pursuing profit is viewed as the natural condition of business, a healthy state that can be dangerously distorted by the introduction of the "political" concerns of government officials. This view goes back at least as far as the presidency of Calvin Coolidge, who famously declared that "the chief business of the American people is business." But his subsequent (and often ignored) statement is perhaps more significant: "They are profoundly concerned with producing, buying, selling, investing and prospering in the world. I am strongly of opinion that the great majority of people will always find these are moving impulses of our life." For Coolidge, business was a substitute for politics, not merely for businesspeople, but for all Americans.

If ordinary people are incipient business owners, then the reverse is also true: businesses are treated as people. This view, which dates back to nineteenth-century jurisprudence and the doctrine of "corporate personhood," has only accelerated in recent years. It is not uncommon for Hobby Lobby to be described as a "Christian" or "faith-based" company, or for the Berkeley-based fast-food restaurant, Top Dog, to be called a "libertarian business."

These designations are a new phenomenon. Although there have always been companies that sold religious products and business titans, such as John D. Rockefeller, who were characterized as Christians, nobody would have described Standard Oil as a "Christian enterprise." While the new nomenclature can be seen as a recognition of the political nature of business, it has been used very differently—as an assertion of identity politics.

It is a measure of the influence of this discourse—and part of a long-term concerted campaign by advocates of "free enterprise"—that Gelles accepts the view that profits are the "natural design" of business and that it is only the recent "duress" that has led businesses to engage in politics. Business leaders have long couched their combativeness as a response to unfair attacks by savvy and effective bureaucrats and politicians armed with highly cultivated political instincts, which businessmen and women supposedly lack. In accepting this conception of apolitical businesspeople forced into politics, recent commentators are recapitulating an old story, one that has been narrated since at least the early days of the New Deal. This narrative was repeated throughout the period from the 1930s through the 1970s, the era that historians refer to as the "New Deal Order." The culmination of this style of argument came in 1971, with a document that has come to be known to history as the "Powell Memo."

Forty-six years ago, the corporate lawyer, Lewis F. Powell, Jr., just months away from being nominated by Richard Nixon for a place on the Supreme Court, wrote a confidential memorandum to the US Chamber of Commerce in which he encouraged current business leaders and trade groups to inject themselves more firmly in politics. In his memo, Powell claimed that what he called "the apathy of business"—its normal state of disengagement from politics—was increasingly untenable. "No thoughtful person can question that the American economic system is under broad attack," Powell wrote. Business needed to respond forcefully, for the "survival of what we call the free enterprise system" was at stake. The old formula, in which business interests "tried to maintain low profiles, especially with respect to political action" was no longer feasible in a new era that called for "hard-nose contest with their critics." If what Powell called "the business system" was to flourish, it would have to get over "a disposition to appease" and stop shunning "confrontation politics," which had, regrettably, become a necessary tool in the battle to save itself and the country.

What was significant about the Powell Memo was not just that it encouraged business leaders and organizations to engage in anti-governmental politics, but that it also counseled them to enter into the culture wars. Powell emphasized that his colleagues should fight in the arena of popular culture. He demanded ideological "balance" on college campuses and in the media (which, he noted, were fundamentally businesses dependent "upon profits, and the enterprise system to survive"). Claiming that the media had puffed up Ralph Nader into a "legend," he called for equal veneration for business leaders. He highlighted the importance of "television, which now plays such a predominant role in shaping the thinking, attitudes and emotions of our people" and devoted a whole section to this topic in a portion of the memo titled "What Can Be Done About the Public?"

In September 1972, after Powell joined the Supreme Court, his confidential memo was made public. The investigative reporter Jack Anderson broke the story of Powell's memo in three of his "Washington Merry-Go-Round" columns, calling it "a blueprint for an assault by big business on its critics," which reflected a "militant political action program." (Anderson lifted the phrase "political action" directly from Powell.) Ever since, commentators have pointed to it as an important turning point in the conservative counterrevolution. The Powell Memo changed America and ignited a right-wing political movement, according to Jerry Landay, in a hyperbolic assessment that is not out of line with the views of many commentators.

But even then, Powell's message that business needed to enter politics was not new. In 1933, soon after Franklin D. Roosevelt became president, one of his leading opponents, Col. Robert R.

McCormick, the editor and publisher of the *Chicago Tribune*, argued that "business must enter politics or be destroyed by radical notions." As McCormick described it, this was an unwanted and purely defensive war. Politics, in the form of the New Deal, imperiled business and therefore business must, against its normal instincts, turn to politics so as to be able to carry out its normal, apolitical functions. Such calls for business leaders to enter politics were echoed throughout the twentieth century.

The Powell Memo is thus best thought of as the culmination of a long-term strategy of fighting—rather than accommodating—the New Deal order, of becoming political only to defeat politicians who were straying outside of their lanes in their attack on business. It was also an extension of the recognition that public relations was a crucial front in the war for free enterprise, a position that advocates of "selling free enterprise" had stressed since the 1930s. With the benefit of historical hindsight, we can observe that Powell wrote his memorandum at a time when the New Deal coalition was under threat. One of the most astute readers of the change in mood was Richard Nixon. In a nationwide radio address in 1968, he announced that a totally different grouping had emerged, one which would take down the last vestiges of the New Deal order. "Without most of us realizing it, a new alignment has been formed," Nixon declared. He called this alignment the "silent center." Nixon's message was not at all new: "The more centralized and domineering a government gets, the less personal freedom there is for the individual." But he argued that this message had a more receptive audience that made up the nation's majority. Nixon was prescient. A decade later, a Gallup poll confirmed increasing agreement with the claim that "the government has gone too far in regulating business and interfering with the free enterprise system."

Business interests won this political battle in large measure by claiming that to reject "politics" as it has become understood at the height of American liberalism. In his memo, Powell highlighted the danger of "stampedes by politicians to support almost any legislation related to 'consumerism' or to the 'environment.'" Powell called for a revival of faith in what he said was "variously called: the 'free enterprise system,' 'capitalism,' and the 'profit system.'" This was the natural business environment, rather than the bureaucratically imposed and therefore political system that threatened to turn the nation in a socialist direction.

Powell imagined a topsy-turvy world in which business had "little influence" in the political arena. On top of its own ineffectuality, business had become, Powell claimed, the "favorite whipping-boy of many politicians for many years." It had, incredibly, sunk to the level of a subaltern group, a hated and despised "other," whose interests were not represented in society's corridors of power. Indeed, Powell claimed that "few elements of American society today have as little influence in government." As evidence, Powell highlighted the widespread condemnation of corporations by that year's presidential candidates. Moreover, Powell observed a growing class war that served to "undermine confidence and confuse the public." He detected in the attacks on free enterprise a new form of "political demagoguery"—which consisted of "setting of the 'rich' against the 'poor,' of business against the people"—as "the cheapest and most dangerous kind of politics." Given business's status as a "whipping-boy," Powell understood these juxtapositions as perverse because it they justified class warfare directed against a group lacking prestige or power.

It is in this context that Milton Friedman's 1970 defense of business's responsibility to produce "profits" is significant. What Gelles takes to be an argument for political neutrality, was, in reality, a manifesto for a counterrevolution against the social control of business through governmental instruments. It was a call for business to reclaim its rightful place as director of its destiny rather than being "unwitting puppets," as he put it, to "the intellectual forces that have been undermining the basis of a free society." Friedman, like Powell, wrote in a highly charged political moment, a time when the consumer advocate, Nader, routinely made Gallup's annual list of most admired Americans and young people were, according to Stewart Alsop (in a passage quoted by Powell) disposed to "despise the American political and economic system" and support the "socialization of basic US industries." In supporting the idea that business should operate according to natural "market mechanisms" rather than "political mechanisms" as "the appropriate way to determine the allocation of scarce resources," Friedman was himself making a political argument masked as an observation about how business worked.

Readers of the Friedman article took him to be making a political argument. They responded that there was nothing natural about profits—that they should be thought of as the product of political debate and discussion. "When we demand that automobiles be designed so as not to foul the air, we are weighing a 1 per cent reduction in corporate profits against a 10 per cent increase in the cost of remaining healthy," argued one of the letters to the *Times* in response to the article. Another reader noted that profit maximization by business forced "society at large to absorb the costs of environmental pollution, rather than internalizing such costs and thereby reducing net profits." In the 1970s, as the New Deal Order waned, business's assertions that profits were neutral and outside of politics were frequently challenged. The recent commentary on businesspeople in politics suggests the need for a revival of such provocations.

Howard Schultz, the chairman of Starbucks, is quoted in Gelles' article praising the recent political awakening of CEOs: "Not every business decision is an economic one." This is undoubtedly true. But what has been obscured in the recent celebrations of the newfound moral voice of business leaders is that economic decisions are also political. In emphasizing a certain type of corporate ethics and hiving off economics from ethical and moral consideration, both business leaders and those writing about them have dangerously narrowed the meaning of politics. In so doing, they have reinforced business leaders' preferred narrative about the nature of business—a story which insulates them from criticism of their actual role as important political actors in all senses of the term.

> *"The theory is that these and other well-financed organizations have coordinated efforts in a conspiracy to commit intellectual fraud against the public in order to protect their financial and political interests."*

Corporations Have the Right to Freedom of Expression

Donald A. Downs

In the following viewpoint, Donald A. Downs considers a promise made by presidential candidate Hillary Clinton in the run-up to the 2016 election (which she lost). Clinton vowed to strike a blow against Citizens United, a law that gives personhood to corporations and allows businesses the ability to donate large sums to political parties and candidates under the guise of freedom of expression. Downs argues that introducing a constitutional amendment to restrict corporate donations is a violation of the First Amendment and the right to free speech. He predicts a "slippery slope" effect would have ensued if Clinton had been successful, whereby free speech rights would be eroded. Donald A. Downs is an American political science professor at the University of Wisconsin–Madison known for his work on the First Amendment.

"Pro/con: Should Citizens United be Overturned?" by Donald A. Downs, *The Seattle Times*, August 26, 2016. Reprinted by permission.

As you read, consider the following questions:

1. Why, according to the viewpoint, would passing an amendment against Citizens United open a Pandora's box?
2. How does the author defend Citizen's United?
3. What should be the government's response to free speech issues, according to the viewpoint?

Hillary Clinton continues to vow that she'll undo the Supreme Court's decision in the 2010 *Citizens United* case, promising to introduce a constitutional amendment restricting corporate campaign activities if elected president.

This would set a dangerous course, eroding the First Amendment guarantee of freedom of expression.

Clinton and other progressives argue that the 5-4 Supreme Court ruling in *Citizens United v. Federal Election Commission* was a decision by the court to allow "big money" to influence elections by giving corporations, unions and other groups the same political speech rights as individuals under the First Amendment. Clinton has even suggested that the court used the case to thwart her previous presidential bid.

It's one thing to criticize *Citizens United* and hope a different court would overrule the decision—the case is controversial, and the court has overruled its own opinions dozens of times in its history.

It is another thing, however, to open Pandora's box by passing a formal constitutional amendment creating a specific limit on free speech.

Clinton's focus on going the amendment route is among a growing and disturbing number of instances in which certain groups of people believe that certain other parties, holding views with which they disagree, are such a threat to society that they should be shut down.

Several left-leaning state attorneys general, for example, are trying to use a 1970 anti-racketeering statute—the Racketeer

Influenced and Corrupt Organizations Act, commonly known as RICO—to silence so-called "climate-change deniers," including energy companies, think tanks, scientists and skeptical media organizations, like the conservative magazine *National Review*.

The theory underpinning the free speech assault is that these and other well-financed organizations have coordinated efforts in a conspiracy to commit intellectual fraud against the public in order to protect their financial and political interests.

The history of free speech is replete with individuals and groups pursuing their own interests, whether financial or philosophical, in the marketplace of ideas. (Think the Rev. Martin Luther King Jr. and the civil rights movement, Samuel Gompers and the labor movement, Jack Welch and General Electric.)

Such pursuit can be productive so long as countervailing forces are available and willing to check and criticize what they claim, leaving the ultimate determination of truth and virtue up to we the people.

Fortunately, such checking and counter-argument have been alive and well thus far.

Allowing this to change, as Clinton proposes, would give one entity—the government—the power to decide the truth for the rest of us.

An obvious slippery slope comes with this move and nothing would prevent this type of precedent from being used against the other side when a new governing coalition comes to power.

Meanwhile, a bigger question looms: Why aren't the mainstream media defending the First Amendment, at least as vigilantly as they defend other rights?

As John Stuart Mill maintained in "On Liberty," even ideas that we believe are 100 percent true need to be challenged in order to keep them vital and open to principled revision. Arguments are always made more credible by having to answer to critics.

In the United States, we don't silence our critics and those with whom we disagree. We fight them with facts and ideas. The heavy hands of government stay out of the fray.

"Citizens United, *by underscoring a
right to pool resources for political
expression, has made it easier for
politically engaged Americans to
influence the political process."*

Citizens United Is Making Politics Better

Tim Cavanaugh

*In the following viewpoint, Tim Cavanaugh argues that while many
in the mainstream media and left-wing politics decried the court
decision in* Citizens United, *the upholding of corporate personhood
has actually improved American politics in numerous important ways.
The author believes that loosened campaign contribution laws made
for a more competitive Republican primary season, freed interest
groups from party dependency, made politics more entertaining,
helped the incumbent president, and enlivened local political races.
Tim Cavanaugh is a journalist and screenwriter based in Alexandria,
Virginia. He is a news editor at the* Washington Examiner.

"Five Ways *Citizens United* Is Making Politics Better," by Tim Cavanaugh, Reason.com and
Reason magazine, March 17, 2012. Reprinted by permission.

As you read, consider the following questions:

1. How, according to the viewpoint, did former president Barack Obama break decorum in his remarks concerning *Citizens United*?
2. How has *Citizens United* injected comedy into politics?
3. How did *Citizens United* help then-president Barack Obama?

After the US Supreme Court's 2010 ruling in the case *Citizens United v. Federal Election Commission* struck down a host of free speech restrictions, the Washington establishment responded with a conniption fit that has been rendered hilarious after only two years of history.

Incumbent politicians, the *New York Times*, a crash of tenured law professors, and even President Barack Obama (in a remarkable breach of State of the Union Address decorum) denounced the decision as a "new weapon" for lobbyists, a "major upheaval in First Amendment law," and an undermining of "the influence of average Americans," not to mention "skeptical and even sarcastic."

But as we enter the second year of the 2012 campaign, it's already clear that removing legal restrictions on the right to petition the government for a redress of grievances has done about what you would expect such a deregulation to do: allowed more voices, issues, and ideas into a political marketplace that nobody—except party bosses and newspapers that have lost their monopolies—could legitimately want to restrict.

Here are just five ways *Citizens United* has opened up the 2012 campaign:

5. More Competitive GOP Presidential Race

Not so long ago—as recently as 2008 in fact—the only non-anointed candidate capable of staying in a primary race over the long haul was Rep. Ron Paul (R-Texas). Hillary Clinton did manage to stay in the primary fight against Barack Obama, but by this point in

2008 most of the Republicans—including this year's front-runner, former Massachusetts Gov. Mitt Romney—were long gone.

That would almost certainly have been the case this year for former House Speaker Newt Gingrich and former Pennsylvania Sen. Rick Santorum, had the Supreme Court voted to uphold campaign speech and finance restrictions in 2010. It's an open question how much the nation's political consciousness is being raised by having Santorum push for pornography bans and Gingrich denounce hedge fund managers for expropriating the surplus labor value of the proletariat. But having both men in the race has forced Romney to defend his positions and explain the many inconsistencies in his record.

4. Freeing Interest Groups from Party Dependency

Imagine a world where union bosses were no longer controlled by the Democrats.

Where Gingrich supporters could ignore the mandates of the Republican National Committee.

Where even Occupy Wall Street could form its own Super PAC.

As either utopian or dystopian visions go, that one may be pretty mild, but it's the world we live in right now, and it's a marginal improvement on the top-down campaigning opponents of *Citizens United* seem to prefer.

Citizens United, by underscoring a right to pool resources for political expression, has made it easier for politically engaged Americans to influence the political process. Single-issue activists, mad-as-hell millionaires, business and labor groups, cats and dogs all have more power now to make their voices heard in politics, without having to seek government approval or coordinate with the major parties.

Campaign Finance Limits

Is money a corrosive force in politics? Should the limits on campaign contributions be eased—or erased altogether?

In a session with Paul Miller fellows, two experts on the nation's complex campaign finance laws differed on the effectiveness of those laws—and whether they should even exist.

Larry Noble, senior director and general counsel of the Campaign Legal Center, detailed the ways in which recent decisions by the US Supreme Court have made it easier for wealthy donors to funnel money to support the candidates and campaigns they favor.

The best known of those cases is *Citizens United v. Federal Election Commission*, a 2010 decision that said the government can't prohibit corporations or unions from making independent expenditures for or against individual political candidates. Other pivotal cases were *SpeechNow.org v. FEC*, a lower court case that paved the way for super PACs, and *McCutcheon v. FEC*, which eliminated aggregate limits on contributions by one donor to multiple candidates.

Because certain kinds of contributions don't have to be reported to the FEC, Noble pointed out that "money is used to influence elections and the true source is not being disclosed."

"The game that's being played right now is hide the donor," he said.

David Keating, president of the Institute for Free Speech, questioned the need for limits or for disclosure rules.

"So-called 'dark money' is a very small percentage of the total," he said, adding that it amounted to less than 4 percent of the total in the 2016 election cycle. "I think it's very unlikely to increase in the future. When you look at it from a donor's view, if you want to influence an election, it's a very wasteful way to go about it."

He also said that the concern over big money in elections is overblown—and that people often forget the underlying issue that limits represent.

"What we're talking about here is the First Amendment right to speak out about our government," he said.

"The Pros and Cons of Campaign Finance Limits," by Chris Adams, National Press Foundation, April 20, 2018.

3. Guaranteed Big Laffs

Politics is to comedy as the surface of the moon is to gardening.

But while the polling place will never be anybody's first choice for d'jever-notice yuks, we can at least expect to enjoy the occasional campaign commercial that is intentionally or unintentionally entertaining.

In this respect, 2012 has so far not really lived up to its apocalyptic reputation, though it has provided a few memorably weird moments.

These include Ron Paul's uncharacteristically butch encapsulation of Americans' disenchantment with entrenched politics and craven politicians:

US congressional candidate Roger Williams' all-ass campaign commercial can't be called "funny" in the classical sense, but it's the most compelling material for political fur fetishists since Carly Fiorina's (probably never-to-be-topped) Demon Sheep spot.

And Santorum's "Rombo" campaign ad raises a question for historians: If he makes it to the White House, will Santorum have himself arrested for threatening to assassinate the president?

2. Good Enough for the President!

"Last week," President Obama told the assembled houses of Congress right after *Citizens United* came down, "the Supreme Court reversed a century of law to open the floodgates for special interests—including foreign corporations—to spend without limit in our elections. Well I don't think American elections should be bankrolled by America's most powerful interests, or worse, by foreign entities. They should be decided by the American people."

Yet last month Obama raised $2 million through his own Super PAC. And this week Obama and the congressional Democrats pooled their resources to form a Super-Duper PAC that the Congressional Budget Office estimates will literally have more money than God.

Obama advisor David Plouffe blames the Republicans and libertarian billionaires for this unfortunate necessity—and the

New York Times has been happy to take Plouffe at his word. But folks of a certain age, who remember candidate Obama's similar about-face on matching-funds spending limits in 2008, know that he is just doing what comes naturally.

And he's right to do so. The president is facing a well-earned loss of confidence, and even though the Republicans have declined to field a strong candidate against him, Obama needs to spend tens of millions of dollars on advertising. Without *Citizens United*, that would not be the case. Obama would be coasting even more easily toward re-election.

1. Shaking Up Local Races

In North Carolina's 13th Congressional District a Super PAC is helping challenger George Holding compete with front-runner Paul Coble. In the Virginia Senate race, Democrat Tim Kaine has managed to stay within shouting distance of Republican front-runner George Allen. Even Rep. Spencer Bachus (R-Alabama), who has been making law since the time of Moses, is facing an unprecedented challenge.

In Colorado, liberal groups have helped to transform the state legislature. In Wisconsin, conservative groups are helping Gov. Scott Walker combat a recall attempt engineered by transnational labor. There's even a Super PAC dedicated to throwing out incumbents.

From union thugs to shotgun-toting grannies to eccentric bazillionaires to self-enchanted soccer dads who just want to warn the world about Joseph Kony, all Americans have important new tools to get their respective messages out. That would have happened with or without the Supreme Court's help. But *Citizens United* applies people power to the calcified sphere of politics. The results so far are as terrifying to incumbents as they are delightful to the rest of us.

> *"If enough people realize how monstrous is the policy of equating fictitious corporate 'persons' with real people, then perhaps gradually public opinion will force a change in the Supreme Court's attitude."*

Corporate Personhood Is an Absurdity

Thomas Storck

In the following viewpoint, Thomas Storck argues that while corporate personhood is a convenient way to handle legal disputes that arise with institutions, actually considering corporations as having rights equal to those of humans makes no sense. He considers the decision to grant corporations personhood to be a "power grab" and notes the inconsistency when constitutional "originalists," such as the late Supreme Court justice Antonin Scalia, make decisions that are not consistent with that philosophy. The author believes that Citizens United *must and eventually will be overturned. Thomas Storck is the author of four books, including* Liberalism: A Critique of Its Basic Principles and Various Forms.

"Corporate Personhood and 14th Amendment Rights," by Thomas Storck, EthikaPolitika. org, May 30, 2012. Reprinted by permission.

As you read, consider the following questions:

1. How did corporate personhood get pushed into law artificially?
2. What distinguishes corporate personhood as a legal convenience and equating a corporation with a legal, breathing human?
3. According to the author, what would potentially lead the Supreme Court to reconsider the personhood of corporations?

One of the demands made by the Occupy Wall Street movement has been the ending of the legal fiction of personhood for business corporations. This desire on the part of the Occupy movement is healthy, but the issue is actually more complicated than might at first appear. For corporate personhood and corporate rights under the Fourteenth Amendment to the United States Constitution are two different things, and the first does not necessarily imply the second.

First let us look at the text of the relevant section of the Fourteenth Amendment:

> Section 1. All persons born or naturalized in the United States and subject to the jurisdiction thereof are citizens of the United States and of the State wherein they reside. No State shall make or enforce any law which shall abridge the privileges or immunities of citizens of the United States; nor shall any State deprive any person of life, liberty, or property, without due process of law; nor deny to any person within its jurisdiction the equal protection of the laws.

This amendment was ratified in the summer of 1868, the second of three amendments enacted after the Civil War to free the slaves and secure their rights as citizens. The reference to "persons born or naturalized" would be, one hopes, clear enough so that no one could ever have imagined that the text refers to anything except natural persons. After all, corporate bodies are neither born nor do they achieve citizenship by naturalization. But this was not what occurred.

In the period during and after the Civil War corporations were beginning their successful attempts to influence state legislatures to grant them privileges unknown to ante bellum corporations. These included the right of a corporation to own stock in other corporations, thus allowing the creation of holding companies, and the passage of general incorporation laws. In the ante bellum era corporations were generally chartered by state legislatures for specific purposes, for example, to operate a steamship or a bridge, for a certain number of years, and usually with other restrictions as well. Of course, in some cases, this grant of state authority was tantamount to a temporary grant of monopoly rights. General incorporation laws, which gradually came into existence in the second half of the 19th century, allowed corporations much more flexibility than they previously had. In such a climate of opinion, it was not surprising that corporations, especially the then powerful railroads, would use their political influence to obtain the ultimate prize, corporate personhood rights under the Fourteenth Amendment.

The odd thing is that the US Supreme Court never really gave such a grant of personhood in any of its decisions. Rather, the statement that the Court considered corporations as persons under the Fourteenth Amendment was inserted into the headnote, or prefatory material, of an 1886 case by the man responsible for compiling and printing the Court's decisions, Bancroft Davis, the court reporter. In the case of *Santa Clara County vs. Southern Pacific Railroad* (118 US 394), Davis, with the concurrence of the Chief Justice, inserted the following into the headnote:

> One of the points made and discussed at length in the brief of counsel for defendants in error was that "Corporations are persons within the meaning of the Fourteenth Amendment to the Constitution of the United States." Before argument Mr. Chief Justice Waite said: The Court does not wish to hear argument on the question whether the provision in the Fourteenth

Amendment to the Constitution, which forbids a State to deny to any person within its jurisdiction the equal protection of the laws, applies to these corporations. We are of opinion that it does.

Although nearly twenty years later the Supreme Court formally stated that headnotes do not have any legal force, by then it was too late. The "ruling" in *Santa Clara* had already been cited more than once and had acquired the status of a precedent. So in this extraordinary and clearly extralegal manner corporations in the United States acquired the personhood and, one by one, the rights granted by the Fourteenth Amendment solely to "persons born or naturalized in the United States."[1]

What is even more outrageous is that those justices and judges, such as Antonin Scalia, who make much of their commitment to "originalism," i.e., to interpreting the Constitution as it was understood by those who wrote it, seem to have no difficulty in acquiescing in the hijacking of the Fourteenth Amendment by corporations and their legal lackeys. This would seem to call into question the honesty of their "originalism."

Although it is ludicrous to grant corporations the rights of natural persons under the Fourteenth Amendment, one can make a distinction between the mere notion of corporate personhood or personality and the absurd notion that corporations are entitled to the rights of natural persons. The former is not necessarily wrong, so long as the crucial distinction between natural and artificial persons is maintained. There are many sorts of corporations, including universities and colleges, other non-profits of all kinds, as well as the ubiquitous business corporation. The legal fiction of treating corporate bodies as persons is a great social convenience, so long as it is remembered that they are not natural persons. For if corporate personhood did not exist, how would one interact legally with a corporate body? If one were to sue a university or college, would it be necessary to sue each and every member of the board of trustees, or perhaps each and every administrator and faculty member? Or could a corporate body engage in legal action without involving each and every member or employee or participant?

ARE CORPORATIONS PEOPLE?

"While the civil rights movements for women, racial minorities, and other oppressed groups have been thoroughly studied, there has been another centuries-long push for equal rights that has remained largely unnoticed," writes … Adam Winkler in his new book, *We the Corporations: How American Businesses Won Their Civil Rights* (Liveright/W.W. Norton, 2018).

Winkler illuminates the long drive by corporations to gain constitutional rights normally afforded to people. His story reveals that, while this effort drew widespread notice with the Supreme Court's 2010 *Citizens United* decision, it originated two centuries earlier. "Corporations do not march on Washington or parade down Main Street with signs," he said. "They have won their rights in the Supreme Court in a quiet revolution."

What, in fact, is a corporation, and why do corporations exist?

The earliest corporations, in ancient Rome, allowed groups of people to pool money and carry on a common activity, such as running a business. Today, a corporation is a legal entity, separate and distinct from its owners. If you slip and fall at Starbucks, you sue the company. You can't sue shareholders like Starbucks' executive chairman Howard Schultz. What's become so controversial is corporations having fundamental rights, like religious liberty and the privilege to influence elections.…

Corporate personhood is a convenient method of organizing legal and social life, and for this reason has been around at least since ancient Rome, where it was explicitly recognized in the law. But any sensible person will realize that although corporate personality is a useful tool, corporations are not natural persons and all their legal rights derive from legislative enactment. In fact, strictly speaking, they are not rights at all, simply legal conveniences granted by a governing authority. The following sums up the traditional view of the legal status of corporations:

> As the corporation is in all respects an artificial person, not only is its possession of a distinct legal capacity derived from the state, but the extent to which that capacity may be legitimately

How is the "corporate rights movement" similar to other civil rights movements in America?

Like other civil rights struggles, corporations sought Supreme Court rulings affirming their rights—and often employed similar strategies. Long before the civil rights movement, corporations engaged in civil disobedience against laws they opposed; launched test cases purposefully designed to expand corporate rights; and hired all-star teams of elite lawyers to pursue novel, groundbreaking lawsuits.

One of those lawyers, Roscoe Conkling, was an illustrious 19th century attorney who deceived the Supreme Court at a key moment. How has this reverberated?

One of the most astonishing stories I tell is of the groundbreaking series of test cases brought by the Southern Pacific Railroad to win the rights of equality guaranteed by the 14th Amendment, which was passed to protect the newly freed slaves. In one, Conkling, who had been on the committee that drafted the amendment, misled the justices into believing that the drafters intended to protect corporations. In another, the justices declined to rule on the corporate rights question, but the court's reporter of decisions wrote that they had—and the case would be cited from then on for recognizing broad rights.

"Are Corporations People? Q&A with 'We the Corporations' Author Adam Winkler," by Joshua Rich, Regents of University of California, March 5, 2018.

exercised is determined by the same authority. It is therefore improper to extend to the corporations all the principles regarding personality which apply to natural persons.[2]

Thus to hold that corporations have free-speech rights, or the right to participate in the political process, as if they were natural persons is an abuse of the legal and social convenience which allows a corporate group to be regarded as a single person.

It is true of course that men have a natural right of association. Speaking of labor unions, Pope Leo XIII noted that if the state "forbids its citizens to form associations, it contradicts the very principle of its own existence…" (*Rerum Novarum*, no. 51.). As I said above, there are many different kinds of corporate bodies, and although the state grants them corporate personality and defines their rights and duties, the law ought to distinguish among them as to which derive their fundamental character from "the natural propensity of man to live in society" (ibid.) and which are merely social conveniences and therefore have their entire "legal capacity derived from the state."

Some might object that these suggestions are against private property rights, but such an objection is certainly not based on the Catholic understanding of property rights. Nor does it even seem congruent with the classical liberal idea of absolute property rights either, since logically these would apply only to natural persons. In fact, it is hard to imagine any reasoned case for why corporations deserve Fourteenth Amendment rights. In any event, in the case of Catholic teaching, Pope Pius XI taught the following in his 1931 encyclical *Quadragesimo Anno*:

> It follows from the twofold character of ownership, which we have termed individual and social, that men must take into account in this matter not only their own advantage but also the common good. To define in detail these duties, when the need occurs and when the natural law does not do so, is the function of the government. Provided that the natural and divine law be observed, the public authority, in view of the common good, may specify more accurately what is licit and what is illicit for property owners in the use of their possessions....
>
> However, when civil authority adjusts ownership to meet the needs of the public good it acts not as an enemy, but as the friend of private owners; for thus it effectively prevents the possession of private property, intended by Nature's Author in His Wisdom for the sustaining of human life, from creating intolerable burdens and so rushing to its own destruction. It does not therefore abolish but protects private ownership, and far from weakening the right of private property, it gives it new strength (no. 49).

We should note, moreover, that Pope Pius is speaking here of the property rights of individuals. So although in the case of a corporation, it is certainly true that the individual incorporators or shareholders do have rights not to have their property seized arbitrarily, this hardly translates into rights of the corporation as such, especially to freedom of speech or freedom to participate in the political process. The individual stockholders already have those personal and political rights, and if they choose to exercise them on behalf of their financial interests, this is undoubtedly their right under the Constitution. But it does not follow that the corporate body itself has any such right. The corporation exists as a mere creature of the law and any of its so-called rights are in fact privileges bestowed upon it by the legislature for the sake of the public good.

Although in these times when the power of corporate finance seems well-nigh omnipotent, there is little prospect of the Supreme Court's changing direction and repudiating the power grab made in 1886, still it helps to inform public opinion on these questions. If enough people realize how monstrous is the policy of equating fictitious corporate "persons" with real people, then perhaps gradually public opinion will force a change in the Supreme Court's attitude of the kind we have seen before. After all, there used to be an adage, the Supreme Court follows the election returns.

Endnotes

1. This account is taken from Ted Nace, *Gangs of America: The Rise of Corporate Power and the Disabling of Democracy*, San Francisco, 2003, which provides a handy overview of the rise and consolidation of corporate power.
2. William C. Morey, *Outlines of Roman Law*, 2d ed., New York, 1914, p. 264.

> *"'If only there were some way to prove that corporations were not people,' lamented the* Daily Show's *Jon Stewart. Maybe, he mused, we could show 'their inability to love.'"*

The Supreme Court Has Dramatically Expanded Corporate Rights

Nina Totenberg

In the following viewpoint, Nina Totenberg looks at the history of corporate personhood, and how, through time, laws evolved that enable corporations to influence political elections. Totenberg provides an overview of the controversial Citizens United *decision. Opponents believe that the decision is dangerous, that it will give corporations undue influence in political matters and breed corruption. Some argue that money is not speech. But the Supreme Court has ruled that the freedom of expression guaranteed in the First Amendment must not be curtailed, and* Citizens United *is now the law of the land. Nina Totenberg is a legal affairs correspondent for National Public Radio who focuses on the United States Supreme Court.*

"When Did Companies Become People? Excavating the Legal Evolution," by Nina Totenberg, National Public Radio, July 28, 2014. Reprinted by permission.

As you read, consider the following questions:

1. How, traditionally, have corporations been important to society?
2. How do some observers distinguish between nonprofit and for-profit corporations with regard to corporate personhood?
3. How have comedians attacked the *Citizens United* decision?

Are corporations people? The US Supreme Court says they are, at least for some purposes. And in the past four years, the high court has dramatically expanded corporate rights.

It ruled that corporations have the right to spend money in candidate elections, and that some for-profit corporations may, on religious grounds, refuse to comply with a federal mandate to cover birth control in their employee health plans.

These are personal rights accorded to corporations. To many, the concept of corporations as people seems odd, to say the least. But it is not new.

The dictionary defines "corporation" as "a number of persons united in one body for a purpose." Corporate entities date back to medieval times, observes Columbia law professor John Coffee, an authority on corporate law. "You could think of the Catholic Church as probably the first entity that could buy and sell property in its own name," he says.

Indeed, having an artificial legal persona was especially important to churches, says Elizabeth Pollman, an associate professor at Loyola Law School in Los Angeles.

"Having a corporation would allow people to put property into a collective ownership that could be held with perpetual existence," she says. "So it wouldn't be tied to any one person's lifespan, or subject necessarily to laws regarding inheriting property."

Later on, in the United States and elsewhere, the advantages of incorporation were essential to efficient and secure economic development. Unlike partnerships, the corporation continued to exist even if a partner died; there was no unanimity required to do something; shareholders could not be sued individually, only the corporation as a whole, so investors only risked as much as they put into buying shares.

By the 1800s, the process of incorporating became relatively simple. But corporations aren't mentioned anywhere in the Constitution, leaving the courts to determine what rights corporations have—and which corporations have them. After all, Coca-Cola is a corporation, but so are the NAACP and the National Rifle Association, and so are small churches and local nonprofits.

"All these truly different types of organizations might come under the label 'corporation,'" Pollman observes. "And so the real difficulty is figuring out how to treat these different things under the Constitution."

In the early years of the republic, the only right given to corporations was the right to have their contracts respected by the government, according to legal historian Eben Moglen.

The great industrialization of the United States in the 1800s, however, intensified companies' need to raise money.

"With the invention of the railroad, you needed a great deal of capital to exploit its purpose," Columbia professor Coffee says, "and only the corporate form offered limited liability, easy transferability of shares, and continued, perpetual existence."

In addition, the end of the Civil War and the adoption of the 14th Amendment provided an opportunity for corporations to seek further legal protection, says Moglen, also a Columbia University professor.

"From the moment the 14th Amendment was passed in 1868, lawyers for corporations—particularly railroad companies—wanted to use that 14th Amendment guarantee of equal protection to make sure that the states didn't unequally treat corporations," Moglen says.

Nobody was talking about extending to corporations the right of free speech back then. What the railroads sought was equal treatment under state tax laws and things like that.

The Supreme Court extended that protection to corporations, and over time also extended some—but not all—of the rights guaranteed to individuals in the Bill of Rights. The court ruled that corporations don't have a right against self-incrimination, for instance, but are protected by the ban on warrantless search and seizure.

Otherwise, as the Cato Institute's Ilya Shapiro puts it, "the police could storm down the doors of some company and take all their computers and their files."

But for 100 years, corporations were not given any constitutional right of political speech; in fact, quite the contrary. In 1907, following a corporate corruption scandal involving prior presidential campaigns, Congress passed a law banning corporate involvement in federal election campaigns. That wall held firm for 70 years.

The first crack came in a case that involved neither candidate elections nor federal law. In 1978 a sharply divided Supreme Court ruled for the first time that corporations have a First Amendment right to spend money on state ballot initiatives.

Still, for decades, candidate elections remained free of direct corporate influence under federal law. Only money from individuals and groups of individuals—political action committees—were permitted in federal elections.

Then came *Citizens United*, the Supreme Court's 5-4 First Amendment decision in 2010 that extended to corporations for the first time full rights to spend money as they wish in candidate elections—federal, state and local. The decision reversed a century of legal understanding, unleashed a flood of campaign cash and created a crescendo of controversy that continues to build today.

It thrilled many in the business community, horrified campaign reformers, and provoked considerable mockery in the comedian classes.

"If only there were some way to prove that corporations were not people," lamented the *Daily Show*'s Jon Stewart. Maybe, he mused, we could show "their inability to love."

Fellow Comedy Central comedian Stephen Colbert tried unsuccessfully to get the question of corporate personhood on the South Carolina ballot, and also formed a superPAC, which asked whether voters would be comfortable letting Mitt Romney date their daughters' corporations.

But there are serious people on both sides of this issue.

Cato's Shapiro sees all corporations, when they spend on political campaigns, as merely associations of like-minded people.

"Nobody is saying that corporations are living, breathing entities, or that they have souls or anything like that," he says. "This is about protecting the rights of the individuals that associate in this way."

Countering that argument are those who note that individuals are perfectly free to give money to candidates with whom they agree, and to spend unlimited amounts independently supporting those candidates. They shouldn't need a corporation to express themselves, the argument goes.

Some critics, like Pollman, see a difference between for-profit and nonprofit corporations. A nonprofit corporation formed to advance particular political views is one thing, she says. A large for-profit corporation is something else entirely.

"There's no reason to believe that the people involved—shareholders, employees, even the directors or managers—have come together for an expressive purpose related to anything other than really what the business is doing," she argues.

And shareholders and employees, Pollman observes, have no real recourse if they disagree with how corporate money is spent in campaigns.

And then there is the money-is-not-speech argument. The problem for First Amendment believers, Moglen says, arises not because they think corporations shouldn't have rights so much as they think money isn't equal to speech.

"And we are now winding up using constitutional rules to concentrate corporate power in a way that's dangerous to democracy," he says.

That, of course, is not how the Supreme Court majority sees its decision. The court has said that because speech is an essential mechanism of democracy, the First Amendment forbids discrimination against any class of speaker.

It matters not, the court said just this year, that some speakers, because of the money they spend on elections, may have undue influence on public policy; what is important is that the First Amendment protects both speech and speaker, and the ideas that flow from each.

Periodical and Internet Sources Bibliography

The following articles have been selected to supplement the diverse views presented in this chapter.

Scott Caselton, "It's Time for Liberals to Get over *Citizens United*," Vox, May 7, 2018. https://www.vox.com/the-big -idea/2018/5/7/17325486/citizens-united-money-politics -dark-money-vouchers-primaries

John Dunbar, "The 'Citizens United' Decision and Why It Matters," *The Center for Public Integrity*, May 10, 2018. https:// publicintegrity.org/politics/the-citizens-united-decision-and -why-it-matters/

Garrett Eps, "Don't Blame 'Corporate Personhood,'" *The American Prospect*, April 16, 2012. https://prospect.org/power/blame -corporate-personhood/

Carson Halloway, "Are Corporations People?" *National Affairs* 44, Summer 2020. https://www.nationalaffairs.com/publications /detail/are-corporations-people

Richard L. Hasen, "The Decade of *Citizens United*," *Slate*, December 19, 2019. https://slate.com/news-and-politics/2019/12/citizens -united-devastating-impact-american-politics.html

Arthur S. Jago and Kristin Laurin, "Corporate Personhood: Lay Perceptions and Ethical Consequences," *Journal of Experimental Psychology: Applied* 23.1, 2017, pp. 100–112.

Nick Kunkle, "Corporations Are People? The Origins of Corporate Personhood," Rocket Lawyer, May 5, 2016. https://www .rocketlawyer.com/blog/corporations-people-origins-corporate -personhood-922071

Rita C. Manning, "Corporate Responsibility and Corporate Personhood," *Journal of Business Ethics* 3.1, 1984, pp. 77–84.

Paul Moreno, "Corporate Personhood's Long Life," *National Review*, December 5, 2019. https://www.nationalreview.com/2013/12/corporate-personhoods-long-life-paul-moreno/

Michael J. Phillips, "Corporate Moral Personhood and Three Conceptions of the Corporation," *Business Ethics Quarterly* 2.4, 1992, pp. 435–459.

Sarah Pruit, "How the 14th Amendment Made Corporations into 'People,'" History.com, June 15, 2018. https://www.history.com/news/14th-amendment-corporate-personhood-made-corporations-into-people

Robert Verbruggen, "How Corporations Won Their Civil Rights," *American Conservative*, July 3, 2018. https://www.theamericanconservative.com/articles/how-corporations-won-their-civil-rights/

Adam Winkler, "'Corporations Are People' Is Built on an Incredible 19th-Century Lie," *Atlantic* March 5, 2018. https://www.theatlantic.com/business/archive/2018/03/corporations-people-adam-winkler/554852

Adam Winkler, "Personhood Actually Limits Corporations' Rights; Ending It Would Be a Mistake," *San Francisco Chronicle*, March 2, 2018. https://www.sfchronicle.com/opinion/article/Corporate-personhood-actually-limits-12721448.php

OPPOSING
VIEWPOINTS®
SERIES

CHAPTER 3

When Does Personhood Begin and End?

Chapter Preface

The abortion debate is, on its surface, a battle between those who want to protect the rights of unborn children and others who believe it is up to women to make choices about their reproductive health. But the conflict is also a war of words. Consider, for example, how each side characterizes itself. Those opposing abortion consider themselves "pro-life," not "anti-abortion." They label their philosophical opponents as "anti-life," "pro-death," "pro-abortion," or at worst, "baby killers." The other side self-identifies as "pro-choice" or as being "for women's reproductive rights," while suggesting that social conservatives are "anti-choice" or "anti-women."

So it is with the "personhood movement," which, in its most narrow definition, refers to the abortion debate and the belief that life—and personhood—begins at conception and that abortion is murder. As Jeannie Suk Gerson sums up the arguments: "On one side, the belief that a fetus is a human being would mean that abortion is a form of murder, which makes the idea that it is a woman's 'choice' callous or nonsensical. On the other side, the belief that the abortion decision belongs in the domain of individual autonomy rests on the assumption that, whatever it is, abortion is *not* the killing of a human being."[1]

In many ways, the anti-abortion movement's co-opting of "personhood" is just another salvo in this war of words, the attempt to define what they believe in and what the other side believes.

Words also figure into end-of-life debates. The notion of personhood at the end of life, often as it is applied to those who are terminally ill, has also taken on a life of its own. Religious conservatives stand fast in their belief that a life must not be ended by artificial means, that only a higher power can decide such matters. Others believe that each person—or the person's family—has the right to decide what end-of-life choices are best. Phrases such as "euthanasia," "physician-assisted suicide," "making a patient comfortable," "death panels," and "mercy killing" are the verbal currency of such arguments.

Physicians who have attempted to promote assisted suicide have generally not been held in high regard. The most famous practitioner, Dr. Jack Kevorkian, served time in prison for his willingness to flout convention and the law, even though his patients were willing participants in his mercy killings. As another example of the power of words, "to kevork" someone is a phrase understood disparagingly to end someone's life mercifully or to commit suicide. The phrase has even made it to the internet's Urban Dictionary of slang.

There is a general discomfort in discussing end-of-life matters that often prevents the dying from getting the care they need, including pain medications. Most people try to avoid confronting their own mortality, and witnessing someone else in the final stages of life is unpleasant at best. But physicians and caregivers are increasingly becoming sensitive to the plight of the dying. While physician-assisted suicide is illegal in most states, terminally ill patients are often "made comfortable," which means that they are given increasingly powerful doses of morphine or other opiates that ease a person into the afterlife. Morphine alleviates a patient's pain, but it also induces respiratory depression, which may hasten death. One can witness this so-called "double effect" of pain medication daily in hospitals worldwide, but ask a physician or nurse about this and they may well be reluctant to talk, as the legality of such actions is questionable. It all goes back to society's discomfort with death. Some countries, such as Canada, are more open about end-of-life practices. Since 2016, Medical Assistance in Dying (MAID) has been legal for the terminally ill as a way to end pain and suffering.

Debates about beginning-of-life and end-of-life issues are difficult to have. Oftentimes, they devolve into shouting matches rather than serious discussions, because birth and death are emotional topics. But societies will not advance in their understanding of life and death until people are able to cast aside emotion and engage in these important issues.

Endnotes

1. "How Fetal Personhood Emerged as the Next Stage of the Abortion Wars," by Jeannie Suk Gersen, *New Yorker*, June 5, 2019.

> *"Those who say an embryo is a person
> cannot be satisfied with just opposing
> abortion. They must be concerned
> about its life—not just the chances of
> its death."*

Personhood Must Not End When Babies Are Born

Sanjayan Rajasingham

In the following viewpoint, Sanjayan Rajasingham argues that while a fetus should be accorded personhood, this concept does not provide a "clinching argument" against abortion. Social realities must be taken into account. Society provides little to no help for many young mothers and therefore forces many to seek abortion as a solution. It is not enough, the author believes, to oppose abortion. One must also support life after birth. Sanjayan Rajasingham is a doctoral candidate at Yale Law School with a focus on constitutional law.

As you read, consider the following questions:

1. According to the author, what abuses do Sri Lankan women face on a daily basis?
2. How does science support the personhood of unborn children, according to the viewpoint?
3. What are three steps the state must take to support personhood for mothers and children?

"Abortion, Women and Personhood," by Sanjayan Rajasingham, Groundviews, September 20, 2017. First published on groundviews.org. Reprinted by permission.

The government's plans to liberalise Sri Lanka's abortion laws has polarised public opinion. Abortion is either supported as a natural extension of a woman's autonomy and right to choose, or is opposed as legalised murder. But is there a path beyond the legalise vs criminalise debate?

Dominance and Choice

Support for abortion is founded on women's dignity, rights and choice[1]—things that many Sri Lankan women are denied each day. They face constant harassment on the bus and the streets. They are the victims of startling levels of domestic violence and abuse. They are constrained about what they can say, wear and do. They are also denied a voice in political, religious and legal institutions. These experiences of women are rooted in a system of male dominance—a system which allows men to police and control the everyday lives and choices of many women.

In a male-dominated reality, allowing women to choose to abort seems a positive step. A pregnancy radically alters her life. If it is outside marriage it leads to exclusion and humiliation. If it is the result of rape or incest, the consequences are worse. How can the law force a woman to go through this?

This question cannot be ignored, especially by men, who are removed from these experiences of domination. Society doesn't force us through daily, casual harassment. It will (wrongly) excuse us of most of the burden of raising a child. Of course, those who are removed from a situation don't necessarily need to be silent—the elderly can share their views on public policy decisions that will outlast them, and those with no chance of higher education can comment on tertiary education. What we do expect, however, is that they listen deeply to both sides, and are open to being changed by hearing from those who are most affected.

Abortion and Personhood

The argument of many opponents of abortion is: "My religion says abortion is wrong, so it must be illegal." While religion has its place in public discourse, this is not it. It cannot be a "knock down" argument for or against a law. In fact, however, I don't think we need to refer to religion to raise critical questions about abortion. I will, instead, centre mine on widely-held convictions about human personhood.

What is personhood about? Consider the idea of equality. Almost everyone would agree that "we are all equal." But, of course, we aren't. We are unequal in our intellectual prowess, in our athletic ability, in our skills and backgrounds. Yet though we are empirically unequal, we say that we are equal—not in capacities or attributes but equal in dignity and worth. If our dignity and value isn't located in our achievements or attributes, then on what grounds do we say are we equal? We are equal because of the type of beings that we are. We are human persons.

Personhood is something we have because of the type of being we are. It is the source of our equality, rights and autonomy.[2] So while abortion is about women's autonomy and dignity, it also raises questions about when personhood begins and when we become bearers of dignity and worth. To answer these questions, we must turn to human biology.[3]

The Science of Sexual Reproduction

In ordinary sexual reproduction, a male sperm penetrates and fertilises a female egg. These two sex cells unite and form an entirely new and distinct organism, initially with a single cell—the zygote. Three things stand out about the zygote or early human embryo. First, the embryo is genetically distinct from any cell of its mother or father, including the sperm and the egg. Second, it is human, in that is has the genetic makeup characteristic of human beings. Third, it is a whole or complete, though immature, organism. The embryo has the "genetic programming" needed to direct its growth towards maturity and survival. It is not simply a part of another organism. Unlike the heart, lungs, or liver of the mother, it plays no functional role in the woman's body. Compare this with the egg and the sperm, which are both functionally and genetically identifiable as parts of the male and female parents. They don't direct their own development—they must either combine with a sperm or an egg, or die.[4]

Science confirms, then, that the embryo is a complete organism, and is also a human organism. But is an embryo a human person? Does it possess dignity and worth?

Who Is a Person?

The embryo is not conscious, is incapable of higher mental functions and cannot survive independently. It has the potential for all this, but it can't immediately exercise these capacities. Does the lack of these capacities mean that an embryo isn't a person?

If personhood depends on being conscious, then those who are asleep, or in reversible comas, are not persons. Yet we agree that they are. If personhood depends on higher mental functions, then Down's Syndrome children, the mentally retarded and late-stage Alzheimer's patients are not persons. Yet we agree that they are. If personhood depends on independence, on the ability to survive without constant care and nutrition, then infants and elderly patients are not persons. Yet we agree that they are. We would agree that someone without all three capacities—an infant with Down's Syndrome lying unconscious in a neonatal care unit—is a person. This is the weakness of a "capacities approach" which says that personhood depends on certain capacities: its implication is that certain humans—the disabled, the old, the weak—are not persons and do not have rights. Yet we all know that they are and they do. And if they, with their lack of capacities, are persons, then there is no reason why an embryo is not.

Some say that birth makes a difference. But why? It cannot be appearance, because appearance is not a measure of personhood. It cannot be a capacity for independent survival because, even after we cut the umbilical cord, an infant is completely dependent on others. What difference does birth make?

A better account of personhood—which both explains our convictions and follows human biology—recognises that human beings have different stages of development. We begin as embryonic human beings, develop into fetal human beings, emerge as infant human beings, grow into adolescent human beings and become adult human beings. But there is no difference in kind between these organisms. There is only a difference in their stage of maturity and immediately exercisable capacities—qualities which are irrelevant to their personhood.

If we believe in autonomy, dignity and rights for all, then we believe in human dignity and worth—and it is our personhood that gives us this worth. If we say that an embryo does not possess human dignity and worth, then we must say the same of some of the weak, the old or the ill. Yet since we accept that the latter have dignity and worth, we cannot deny it to the human embryo. The embryo is, therefore, a bearer of human dignity and worth.

Philosophy and Rights

Now some will say that this is just technical, abstract philosophy that ignores the realities that women face. It gives a "clump of cells" a priority that we know intuitively that they should not have. There is weight behind this view. After all, we can see the thirteen-year-old who doesn't understand rape, and can't imagine a pregnancy, but will soon be a mother. We can hear from women who are dying because they used wire clothes hangers to induce abortions. We can meet women who have had to give up their dreams because a narrow-minded society cannot accept their pregnancy. Against all this, how can the embryo have any significance?

Let me say first that an embryo being a person is not, for me, a "clinching argument" against abortion. The law must take social realities into account. Also, while personhood may be philosophical and moral, so are autonomy, dignity, choice and patriarchy. This doesn't detract from the immense practical significance of any of these philosophical and moral ideas. Finally, it is true that women's suffering is tangible and real. By contrast, the embryo is foreign, removed, and barely recognisable to us as human. It's easy to reduce it to a "clump of cells." Yet the foreignness and distance of an embryo's experiences is no reason to reduce the significance of those experiences. If we do that, we are no different from men who dismiss male harassment of women as "harmless banter" or to the rich who dismiss structural poverty as "laziness."

The Law and Compromise

The law is often about messy compromise. An embryo being a person does not mean that the choice and rights of women are unimportant. But it does reframe how we think about the exercise of those rights.

First, it means that abortion is not just about the woman's right to choose. It is about choice in the context of two persons, a woman and an embryo. And in any case, there is no such thing as an "unrestricted right to choose." Everything depends on who is choosing and what they are choosing. Even in liberal theory, our freedom is limited by the rights and freedoms of others. If the embryo is a person, then it is an "other," a bearer of rights. And we treat persons with enormous significance. A pregnancy transforms a woman mentally, physically, emotionally and economically. But is this enough of a reason to end the life of a person?

There are many persons whose existence radically alters our lives. Think of an adult child caring for an aging, incapacitated and increasingly senile parent. Think of parents living with the emotional and mental strain of extricating a teenager out of gang violence. These persons inflict immense emotional, psychological and physical costs on those who care for them. Yet this doesn't mean we may kill them. Similarly, a woman's right to choose is necessarily restricted by the personhood of an embryo.

However, there are always exceptions. We recognise that persons are important, but we also know that there are times— in self-defence and war, for example—where the law allows us to end a person's life. Is abortion sometimes like this? What about a pregnancy following a rape?

A rape leaves its victims shattered. If it leads to pregnancy then a woman has a daily reminder of a horror she wants to escape. If she gives birth our society will heap indignity and stigma on her and the child for the rest of their lives. Isn't this a form of socially mediated torture? Would we judge a torture victim for killing her torturer? Here, of course, the embryo is not responsible for the torture—but neither is the woman. The rapist, and our society, are. What if the only way for a torture victim to end her suffering was to kill an innocent human being? Would we insist she had to bear her suffering?

The experiences of women who have faced this decision shows us that this is a genuine moral dilemma. If we agree that this is an instance where a woman should be free to choose, we must be aware of what this means. It's not just "maximising choice." It means that women who are pregnant because of rape are sometimes subject to socially mediated torture which is so severe that many of them feel that ending the life of an innocent person is the only escape. This says far more about our society than it does about the woman who chooses to abort.

But there are also broader issues at stake. Abortion means changing the medical profession from one which, at least in theory, fights death, to one which actively brings it about. Do we want this? Also, as Dinesha Samararatne argues persuasively, the overwhelming majority of today's abortions are not in the context of rape.[5] They are carried out by married women because they lack knowledge about effective contraception. Why are the new reforms ignoring this reality? Are these proposals, perhaps, a "first step" to normalise abortion, and will they be followed later by more changes? The personhood of an embryo demands that we reflect on these questions.

From Abortion to Pregnancy

The implications of an embryo's personhood go further, however. If it is a person, and persons have significance, then why does our society put most of the responsibility of bearing and raising a child on women? Shouldn't men, and society, play a role? The personhood of an embryo must change how we view pregnancy and not just abortion. Let me suggest three legal responses that go beyond the criminalise/decriminalise debate.

First, we must amend the Penal Code so that women are not subject to criminal sanctions for seeking an abortion. We know that they are often driven to it by forces beyond their control. We also know that a fear of prosecution keeps women from seeking medical assistance when complications occur after an unsafe abortion. This is one way for the law to recognise this.

Second, the law must share the burden of caring for a child more equally. The Maintenance Act of 1999 compels a man who impregnates a woman to maintain her during and after the pregnancy, regardless of whether they are married, with the threat of criminal sanctions. Why not go further and use this moment to introduce a mandatory legal requirement for all government and private institutions to offer paternity leave, with incentives to those who choose to take it? The normative impact of this on how our culture views parenting could be enormous.

Finally, there must be a system of State support—including financial and psycho-social care—for indigent parents and pregnant mothers. This is how the law can respond to the reality of poverty and its impact on women and families. Running a workable system in a culture that shames single-parents is a tremendous challenge. But it is a step towards society bearing more of the responsibility of pregnancy.

Those who say an embryo is a person cannot be satisfied with just opposing abortion. They must be concerned about its life—not just the chances of its death. Those who accept that there are the forces that dominate women, must confront them and create viable alternatives for women who feel that abortion is the only option.

These are things that anyone can support, regardless of their view of abortion. But those who are vocally against abortion, must be vocally in favour of this.

The Law and Beyond

In the end, however, the law has its limits. It can't stop people from shaming raped women. It can't stop people from believing that women are primarily responsible for raising a child. It can't dismantle a system of male domination. It can help, but these are problems of society and culture and they need a response from the members of this society.

Many who recognise the personhood of an embryo fail to be consistent about their convictions. If we oppose abortion because "the law must protect the weak and the marginalised" are we also concerned about the others who are vulnerable in our society? If we believe that those born with deformities are of equal worth, is this reflected in how we treat the disabled in our spheres of influence? If we believe that a child has value regardless of the circumstances of its birth, and a woman regardless of what she has gone through, then how do we treat children born of rape and their mothers? Would we support institutions like PremNivasa or Ma Sevana which work with them?[6] Or are we a part of a system that shames them and makes them feel that abortion is the only option?

If men oppose abortion because of the worth of an unborn child, are we willing to take an equal burden in caring for our children? Would we, for instance, be willing to give up our careers to raise them, rather than expecting our wives to? If we agree that women are marginalised by a system of male control, how can we respond? Would we be willing, for instance, to have awkward conversations and challenge our friends and colleagues about male harassment of women?

Abortion, then, must lead us to ask questions about our own lives. It must also lead us to ask the basic questions about humanness and society. Who is a person? How do we account for our belief in human dignity and worth from? What sort of society do we want to live in? One where the weak and marginalised are protected and valued or one where only the familiar, the connected and those with a voice are heard?

These are difficult questions, but we must face them. For it is only in answering them, and in living our answers, that we can become a society that protects the dignity, autonomy and worth of all persons—whether born or unborn.

Endnotes

1. "Decriminalise abortion in Sri Lanka: Statement by Human Rights Defenders and Women's Groups" DailyFT, 13 September 2017. http://www.ft.lk/opinion /Decriminalise-abortion-in-Sri-Lanka–Statement-by-human-rights-defenders -and-women-s-groups/14-639448
2. Article 1 of the Universal Declaration of Human Rights. In saying this I am not denying that animals and other living beings have their own dignity and worth. I agree that they do.
3. I deliberately avoid dealing with cloning and in vitro fertilisation, though I think that the same conclusions apply.
4. See further Robert P. George and Christopher Tollefsen, *Embryo* (Doubleday 2008) 27-56
5. Dinesha Samararatne, "The Abortion Debate: Mismatched and Misplaced?" Groundviews, 13 September 2017. www.groundviews.org/2017/09/13/the -abortion-debate-mismatched-and-misplaced/
6. See "Events related to PremNivasa," http://www.queenofangels.lk/index .php?act=prem; "Ma Sevana – Home for Teenage Mothers," https://www .sarvodayasuwasetha.org/homes/cdc-for-teenage-mothers-ma-sevana

> *"The distinctions between moral personhood, legal personhood and constitutional personhood are significant. The terms cannot be used interchangeably, lest the entire dialogue be rendered incomprehensible and meaningless."*

There Are Distinctions Between Moral, Legal, and Constitutional Personhood

Americans United for Life

In the following viewpoint, Americans United for Life examines three different types of personhood in order to justify its anti-abortion argument. These three types are moral, legal, and constitutional personhood. The authors suggest that an entity may be defined by one, two, or all three of these definitions. Distinguishing between these three definitions, and not using them interchangeably, is central to its argument that the lives of the unborn must be protected. Even without constitutional personhood, the lives of the unborn can be defended through legal personhood. Americans United for life advances the human right to life in culture, law, and policy.

"What Exactly Is 'Constitutional Personhood'? The Definition of Personhood and Its Role in the Life Debate," Americans United for Life, April 23, 2010. Reprinted by permission. https://aul.org/2010/04/23/what-exactly-is-constitutional-personhood-the-definition-of-personhood-and-its-role-in-the-life-debate/

As you read, consider the following questions:

1. How does the viewpoint distinguish between three types of personhood?
2. How is this distinction, according to the author, central to the debate about abortion?
3. How can an anti-abortion amendment serve as the culmination of personhood arguments?

The debate over legislation and voter initiatives defining state constitutional "personhood" to include the unborn from conception (commonly referred to as "Human Life Amendments," or "HLAs") has sparked significant interest both inside and outside the pro-life community. An overarching goal of the pro-life movement is to protect the innocent lives of unborn persons, and state HLAs have been suggested as one possible means to achieve this goal. However, the media and many advocates on both sides of the abortion debate are not clear about the meaning and effect of the various forms of "personhood." Consequently, it has become difficult to engage in an effective discussion of the personhood of the unborn and various methods or tools for securing legal protection of the unborn.

To facilitate and improve the on-going dialogue on the question of personhood, this article (1) clearly defines and distinguishes the terms "moral person," "legal person," and "constitutional person"; (2) points out how problems will arise from a lack of understanding of the differences between these terms; and (3) discusses the significance of these distinctions in the context of the debate on life issues.

The Moral Person

Thinking of the term "moral person" brings to mind the notion of the moral agent. The moral agent, generally speaking, is a being that is capable of knowing the difference between good and evil; is capable of making moral judgments based on this knowledge;

can choose to engage in, and does engage in, good and evil actions; and can be held responsible for the good or evil actions engaged in. The moral person, in other words, is a rational being. However, is moral personhood conferred merely by having a rational nature, or by actual engaging in rational activities?

According to the traditional definition, (moral) personhood is something that a human being has simply because he/she is a human being with a rational nature, regardless of whether or not rational activity ever takes place. The classical philosophical definition of (moral) person was provided by Boethius:

> *Person is an individual substance of rational nature.* As individual it is material, since matter supplies the principle of individuation. The soul is not person, only the composite is. Man alone is among the material beings person, he alone having a rational nature. He is the highest of the material beings, endowed with particular dignity and rights.[1] (Emphasis added)

However, John Locke presented a different (modern) approach to (moral) personhood. According to Locke, a person is "a thinking intelligent Being, that has reason and reflection, and can consider itself as itself, the same thinking thing in different times and places; which it does only by that consciousness, which is inseparable from thinking, and as it seems to me essential to it."[2] For Locke, personhood is not dependent on merely having a rational nature; rather, it is dependent on the actual use of reason.

In short, classical philosophy treats all members of the human species as (moral) persons, whereas in modern philosophy, not all members of the human species qualify as (moral) persons.

The Legal Person

Unlike moral personhood, legal personhood is conferred by positive (or "man-made") law. Positive law comes in two forms: common law and statutory law. A legal person is an entity that is recognized and protected under common law or statutory law. More specifically, a legal person is an entity who can, under common law or statutory law, hold and sell property, and sue or be sued.

It is clear that one does not need to be a member of the human species to be a legal person—corporations, law firms and schools are legal persons, although not human. Furthermore, not all members of the human species are legal persons—born and unborn children are not legal persons in some circumstances. In this way, the definition of "legal personhood" is in part informed by Locke's theory of personhood (that not all humans are persons).

The category of legal personhood encompasses limited portions of two separate and distinct spheres: humans and non-humans. The definition of legal personhood extends to a limited segment of humans, and to a limited segment of non-humans (e.g., it extends to legally-formed corporations, but not to plants).

History of Legal Personhood

Historically, the most significant law that protected the sanctity of human life was homicide law. By definition, it prohibited the killing of a human being as a human being, strictly speaking, without explicitly referring to the human being as a person. Today, as a practical matter, fetal homicide laws and wrongful death laws do protect the life of the unborn child as a human being. Moreover, wrongful death laws protect the unborn child as a "person," since wrongful death laws protect persons as persons. The role of legal personhood in the life debate shall be discussed in further detail in the sections to follow.

The Constitutional Person

A broad definition of "constitutional personhood" is the status of a human being or legal entity with some or all constitutional rights. Constitutional rights are normally protected against governmental (or state) action. "Persons" are protected in the US Constitution in the Fifth and Fourteenth Amendment, from governmental (state or federal) action. In the abortion context, however, the term "constitutional personhood" typically refers to whether the unborn child is protected by the Constitution or, more specifically, by the Fourteenth Amendment. The Fourteenth Amendment protects "persons," but the US Supreme Court in *Roe v. Wade* in 1973 held that that term does not include the unborn child. Thus, the unborn child is not a "constitutional person" within the meaning of the Fourteenth Amendment, due to the Court's interpretation in *Roe v. Wade*."

Problems with Failure to Recognize the Difference Between the Definitions of "Personhood"

The distinctions between moral personhood, legal personhood and constitutional personhood are significant. The terms cannot be used interchangeably, lest the entire dialogue be rendered incomprehensible and meaningless.

To provide a brief explanation of why the terms cannot be substituted for one another, consider the following: A legal person is sometimes, but may not always be a moral person (e.g., a corporation is not a moral person). A moral person is sometimes, but may not always be a legal person (e.g., a born child cannot sell property). A legal person is sometimes, but may not always be a constitutional person (e.g., a corporation does not have a constitutional right to protection against self-incrimination). A constitutional person is sometimes, but not always a legal person. A constitutional person is sometimes, but may not always be a moral person (e.g., a corporation is not a moral person). Lastly, a moral person is sometimes, but may not always be a constitutional person (e.g., an unborn child is not a constitutional person).

It is clear that if the various types of "personhood" are used interchangeably, the entire conversation would simply not make sense!

Understanding the Different Roles of Legal and Constitutional Personhood in the Life Debate

It has been demonstrated that one need not be a constitutional person to be a legal person; in other words, "personhood" does not need to be defined in the Constitution for a human being to have legal protection. Evidence supporting this conclusion can be drawn directly from the life debates. For example, state and federal protections for unborn victims of violence (also known as "fetal homicide laws") treat the unborn as legal persons by treating the killing of an unborn human as a form of homicide. Hence, the unborn are protected in law in certain instances, even without constitutional personhood.

It is also important to note that, even if an unborn person is given constitutional personhood by means of an HLA, that unborn person is not necessarily a legal person protected by criminal homicide laws. This is because the Constitution only applies to actions of the US Government, and not actions by individual persons. The creation of constitutional personhood for the unborn will not stop abortion providers from killing unborn children by abortion. Only a criminal homicide law that establishes legal personhood for the unborn could stop abortion providers from killing the unborn through abortion. In other words, an HLA by itself would not be an effective way to provide comprehensive protection for the unborn.

However, this is not to say that constitutional amendments are uniformly not a prudent path. For example, if an activist state supreme court enshrines *Roe* in a state constitution, adopting a tightly drafted amendment that is tailored to that decision with the specific intent to correct the decision would be the only way to address the situation. Moreover, a personhood amendment is not the only kind of constitutional amendment that can counter *Roe*. For example, an alternate amendment could be one that establishes that "no right to abortion is protected by the constitution."

It is important to remember that constitutional amendments come at the end of a series of legal and social reform, not at the beginning. They are the "crowning achievement" of a record of legislative and cultural changes, rather than the catalyst that begins such change. Amendments have historically functioned as "reinforcers" of already-existing legal policies and cultural values. The history leading to the adoption of the 13th Amendment and 19th Amendment are perfect examples of this principle and historical trend.

Conclusion

In short, the media and others engaging in the life debate need to recognize the distinctions between the definitions of moral personhood, statutory and common law personhood and constitutional personhood, and they must not use the terms interchangeably. Increased awareness must be given to the fact that the unborn are protected in law in certain circumstances without constitutional personhood. In addition, there must be increased awareness that a human life amendment would not apply to individual abortion providers and would not afford the unborn legal statutory personhood. The public must know that there are many ways to protect the sanctity of human life aside from an amendment to the Constitution that would create constitutional personhood for the unborn, and also take away the abortion issue from the states. This awareness requires an understanding of the various forms and definitions of personhood, and an openness to considering all feasible and effective ways to protect human life. Once this awareness is achieved, only then can a comprehensible and effective dialogue on human personhood take place.

Endnotes

1. *De Persona et Duabus Naturis*, ii, iii, in P.L., LXIV, 1342 sqq.
2. *Essay on Humane Understanding*, Book 2, Chapter 27, Section 9.

"As a society, do we believe that there
is a point in pregnancy where women
lose their civil rights?"

Fetal Personhood Should Not Come at the Expense of the Mothers

Terry Gross

In the following viewpoint, a series of interviews conducted by Terry Gross, the question of whether mothers can be criminally charged for their actions while pregnant, particularly drug abuse, is considered. While some believe the rights of fetuses are beginning to supersede those of the mother, perhaps as a result of a longtime campaign to re-criminalize abortion by anti-abortion groups, others believe that mother and unborn child should not be treated as adversaries, but as a partnership, and that what is good for one is also good for the other. Putting women in prison or otherwise punishing them for bad choices does nothing to advance the child's potential outcomes. Terry Gross is the longtime host of National Public Radio's program Fresh Air.

"Personhood in the Womb: A Constitutional Question," whyy.org, National Public Radio Inc. (NPR), November 21, 2013.Reprinted by permission.

As you read, consider the following questions:

1. How does Lynn Paltrow advance the cause of pregnant mothers?
2. How does Barbara Mason argue for the rights of unborn children?
3. How does Dr. Barbara Levy strike a balance between the two sides?

Should a pregnant woman whose behavior has been deemed dangerous to her fetus be legally punished or forced into medical procedures against her will? A study released earlier this year found hundreds of cases across the country where pregnant women were arrested and incarcerated, detained in mental institutions and drug treatment programs, or subject to forced medical interventions, including surgery.

The study, conducted by the group National Advocates for Pregnant Women, found 413 criminal and civil cases where law enforcement intervened in the lives of pregnant women between 1973—the year the Supreme Court ruled in *Roe v. Wade*—and 2005.

Fresh Air's Terry Gross speaks with the group's executive director, Lynn Paltrow, who says the legal claims used to justify some of these actions rely on the same arguments that are made in support of personhood measures that would grant the fetus full constitutional rights independent of the pregnant woman. Gross also speaks with Jennifer Mason of Personhood USA, a leader in the personhood movement.

And she speaks with Dr. Barbara Levy, the American Congress of Obstetricians and Gynecologists' vice president for health policy, about related medical issues.

Interview Highlights

Lynn Paltrow, of National Advocates for Pregnant Women

On the case of Alicia Beltran, a pregnant woman in Wisconsin who was forced into a residential drug treatment program

"In Ms. Beltran's case, what happened was she confided in her doctor about her past drug use. By the time she started with a new OB-GYN when she was approximately 12 weeks pregnant, she had stopped all use of any drugs, and yet, the next thing she knew ... five law enforcement officials were at her home. They arrested her, they put her in handcuffs, they took her to an emergency room where she was examined, and that examination said she looks fine, the baby looks fine. Nevertheless, they put her in jail; they put her in leg shackles; they took her to a courtroom where there was already a lawyer appointed for her 12-week fetus. And she was not herself entitled to a lawyer. And the judge, the commissioner ordered her into a residential treatment program for 90 days that did not even provide the treatment that people were saying she needed."

On the Wisconsin law that allowed for Beltran's arrest

"It's in the civil children's code, and it permits ... pregnant women who habitually lack self-control in the use of drugs or alcohol to be taken into immediate custody only on reasonable suspicion.

Many prosecutors in many states, however, have arrested women based on the claim that they were pregnant and used a criminalized drug, arguing that the state's child abuse law should be interpreted to apply to fertilized eggs, embryos and fetuses, and give police officers and others authority over pregnant women.

And what our research shows is that they argue that the word "child" in these statutes ought to be interpreted as giving the state power over pregnant women from the moment they conceive. And what they rely on for that interpretation is very often post-*Roe v. Wade* anti-abortion statutes that make declarations of separate rights for fertilized eggs, embryos and fetuses. State feticide laws that are passed, usually in the wake of extreme violence against pregnant women, they're passed saying that it will provide protection to pregnant women and their unborn children, and then it's turned around and used by prosecutors to justify the arrest of pregnant women themselves."

On the movement to grant full legal rights to fetuses

"The personhood movement is working to have fertilized eggs, embryos and fetuses recognized as completely separate constitutional persons under the law. It's not only [Personhood USA], it's 40 years of efforts by a variety of organizations who seek to recriminalize abortion.

If it succeeds and fertilized eggs, embryos and fetuses are recognized as separate persons under the law, then what happened to Alicia Beltran in Wisconsin could happen, theoretically, to any pregnant woman. ... You could essentially have every pregnant woman subject to a person who is entitled to her medical records, who is entitled to require her to undergo whatever medical procedure is best for her, have her arrested if she doesn't obey.

The question all of these cases pose—the question that the Personhood USA really raises—is: As a society, do we believe that there is a point in pregnancy where women lose their civil rights?"

Jennifer Mason, of Personhood USA
On what legal rights she would like a fetus to have

"The basic rights to life, liberty and the pursuit of happiness. You know, the 14th Amendment requires equal protection under the law for everybody, and so we believe that every human being, regardless of their location, whether they're in the womb or out of it, deserves those protections and those rights."

On punishing pregnant women who use drugs

"I think it is appropriate to treat the case just like you would a case where a woman is giving drugs to a newborn in the home. Children that are addicted to drugs when they are born go through terrible withdrawals. The womb should be the safest place for babies and should not be subject to poison just because they're located in the womb. ...

I do believe that anybody using illegal drugs should be reported. There should be consequences for breaking the law. I think to give pregnant women a pass just because they're pregnant when anyone else injecting drugs into a child would be prosecuted would be wrong."

Barbara Levy, of the American Congress of Obstetricians and Gynecologists

On the effects on the fetus of the women using opioid drugs during pregnancy

"We know of no long-term consequences. We have looked. There's been one long-term study looking at infants that were exposed to opioids, looking at their cognitive development, how their brains work, and how they're functioning up to five years of age, and have not seen any difference between those babies and unexposed children. ...

The placenta filters a lot of this, so the amount that gets to the baby is far less than what you're seeing in the mother's circulation, and so it's not surprising that chronic exposure to a very low amount of a medication wouldn't have a significant effect long term."

On her concerns about women being forced into the criminal justice system for abusing drugs during pregnancy

"From the medical standpoint, abruptly discontinuing some of these medications, particularly opioids, but others, can result in very negative outcomes for the baby. They can result in premature labor. They can result in fetal distress, meaning that the baby's not getting adequate oxygen, and they can even result in fetal death. So attributing the very best of intentions to folks that are developing these laws, the unintended consequences may be that the babies have more negative effects than if we allowed proper treatment for these women.

The fundamental concern that I have is that we're criminalizing a medical problem that these women suffer from, and that we don't do that to any other segment of our society. I understand the concern about the unborn fetus, but the very best way to manage that situation and the very best outcome for the unborn fetus is to treat the mom and the baby as a unit, and to get the best care for the mom. That means she has to be comfortable and free to seek care without concern that she will be placed in jail."

> "The psychology of illness is the psychology of loss…. When you're a little ill, you encounter inconvenience or annoyance. When you're very ill, you start to lose your sense of self, your sense of person. There's a notion of no longer feeling like who you were."

Health Caring Is an Important Part of Health Care

Meg Barbor

In the following viewpoint, Meg Barbor argues that "health caring," or empathy, is as much a component in successful treatment of cancer patients as health care itself. Severe or terminally ill patients not only lose their health, they lose their sense of self. They face an existential crisis. To counter such pessimism, physicians need to treat their patients with dignity and respect. Affirming a patient's personhood is an important factor in good health care. No one wants to be reduced to his or her illness. The more health care providers know about the whole patient, the more they are inclined to treat the patient with dignity and respect. Meg Barbor is a master of public health and has written about a wide variety of public health issues.

"Dignity, Personhood, and the Culture of Medicine," by Meg Barbor, HSP News Service, L.L.C., August 15, 2014. Reprinted with permission from The ASCO Post. Copyright 2014. Harborside.

As you read, consider the following questions:

1. What is the difference between "health care" and "health caring"?
2. How does the Patient Dignity Question help affirm a patient's personhood?
3. Which health care providers tend to be more empathetic to patients?

Cancer patients need more than good health care: they need health caring, according to palliative care specialist Harvey M. Chochinov, MD, PhD, Distinguished Professor of Psychiatry at the University of Manitoba and Director of the Manitoba Palliative Care Research Unit, CancerCare Manitoba.

Health care pertains to cognition, knowledge, technical procedures, and prowess, whereas health caring pertains to things that are going to cause patient satisfaction or dissatisfaction, explained Dr. Chochinov during the Plenary Session at the 2014 Multinational Association of Supportive Care in Cancer/International Society of Oral Oncology (MASCC/ISOO) Symposium, held recently in Miami.

"We have a system designed to provide health care as distinct from a system that is about health caring," he said. "Like our patients, we need to see ourselves as vulnerable.... There is very little that separates us from our patients other than time and luck.... And if we can see ourselves in that way, we are more likely to be able to practice caring and compassionate medicine," he suggested.

The idea of health caring is the gateway to disclosure. When patients feel that caring is present and that they matter as a whole person, they're much more likely to be forthcoming with their physicians. This disclosure leads to greater honesty and a greater likelihood that treatment plans will be consistent with patients' goals of care, he said.

The Dignity Model

Dr. Chochinov and colleagues published a study in 2006 that examined dignity in the terminally ill in a population of 211 patients with end-stage cancer and less than a 6-month life expectancy.[1] Patients were given a list of variables and asked which issues would have an influence on their sense of dignity. For nearly 75%, "no longer feeling like who you were" was found to be a profound dignity-related and existential issue.

"The psychology of illness is the psychology of loss," he explained. "When you're a little ill, you encounter inconvenience or annoyance. When you're very ill, you start to lose your sense of self, your sense of person. There's a notion of no longer feeling like who you were."

Other important issues cited by patients and associated with sense of dignity were "feeling a burden to others" and "not being treated with respect or understanding."

Respect and Understanding

"We need to think of ourselves as people who are in a position to provide affirmation. That's not a word frequently used in health care, but it's an important word," he emphasized.

"The irony is that we spend our entire professional lives studying how to look after patients, when the reality is that no one wants to feel like just a patient," he said. The issue of affirmation is the ability to see patients as whole human beings. The notion of respect is something that clinicians can provide or withhold, he added.

Ten years ago, in an article titled "Dignity and the Eye of the Beholder," Dr. Chochinov explored the notion of how patients perceive themselves as seen by others.[2] He asserted that patients figuratively look into the eyes of health-care providers for a reflection that will either affirm or disaffirm their sense of person.

"If they only see their illness, they feel that they have been reduced to their ailment and nothing else has registered. On the other hand, if they see that the reflection in the eye of the beholder is one that contains a picture of the entire person—not just the patient—they feel affirmed," he suggested.

Patient Dignity Question

Seeing patients in a way that affirms their dignity and personhood is of utmost importance. According to Dr. Chochinov, the easiest and most straightforward way to put personhood on the clinical radar is to ask patients, "What should I know about you as a person to help me take the best care of you that I can?" Dr. Chochinov and colleagues coined this the Patient Dignity Question, or PDQ, due to the positive correlation between affirming personhood and preserving dignity.

Dr. Chochinov and colleagues examined the importance and significance of this question to patients, family members, and health-care providers in a study.[3] They found that nearly all patients wanted their answers to the Patient Dignity Question to be included on their charts, and in many cases they wanted copies for themselves or family members. Nearly all participants felt their answers had been accurately represented, deemed this information important for health-care providers, thought this information could affect their health care, and would recommend use of the Patient Dignity Question for other patients and families.

When health-care providers were asked about the influence of the information gathered from the Patient Dignity Question, the vast majority said they had learned something new about their patients. Over half said they were emotionally affected by the information and felt it had changed their attitude. The majority said it had influenced their care or sense of respect, empathy, and their sense of connectedness with that individual.

In general, female practitioners were more likely to be responsive to issues surrounding personhood than their male counterparts. Additionally, health-care providers with the most experience were most likely to be open to issues of personhood, followed by those with no experience at all.

"This is likely due to the fact that those with the most experience know the importance of personhood," Dr. Chochinov suggested, "and those with no experience—students—had the humility to know how little they actually knew."

Endnotes

1. Chochinov HM, Krisjanson LJ, Hack TF, et al.: Dignity in the terminally ill: Revisited. *J Palliat Med* 9:666-672, 2006.
2. Chochinov HM: Dignity and the eye of the beholder. *J ClinOncol* 22:1336-1340, 2004.
3. Chochinov HM, McClement S, Hack T, et al.: Eliciting personhood within clinical practice: Effects on patients, families and healthcare providers. Under review.

> "We are doing still too little to have
> a significant government impact on
> suicides, and we are doing even less
> for the elderly because we continue to
> consider the elderly as less important
> than young people."

Elderly Suicides Have Increased

Paul Donoughue

In the following viewpoint, Paul Donoughue writes about the growing problem of suicide among Australia's elderly population. Donoughue cites numerous examples of older Australians giving up on their lives due to their perceived worthlessness in society. As the elderly begin to lose their sense of personhood and self worth, there is a tendency to give up on life. Living alone is a key indicator for depression among elder adults. Not being able to do basic tasks is another. Cultures that value older adults less than young people also tend to promote suicides among the elderly. Paul Donoughue covers music and popular culture for the Australian Broadcasting Corporation's (ABC) news website and has contributed to the Guardian, Good Weekend, *the* Australian, *and other publications.*

"Why Are Elderly Australians Taking Their Own Lives?" by Paul Donoughue, ABC.net, October 4, 2016. Reprinted by permission.

As you read, consider the following questions:

1. Why does Donoughue consider elderly suicide an epidemic?
2. What factors lead elderly adults to take their own lives?
3. How, according to Donoughue, could Australia do better in preventing such suicides?

Last Christmas Eve, at a dementia care facility in suburban Sydney, Steve Atkins' 93-year-old mother decided her time had come. Her son had recently told her he would not be spending Christmas Day with her. It was not her first attempt, nor was it without forewarning.

"When she was told she was going into care, and her GP told her that, she immediately said 'I will kill myself,'" Mr. Atkins said recently at a cafe in central Sydney.

Mona Atkins has two different kinds of dementia and also suffers from bipolar, undiagnosed for much of her life. She spent about two weeks in hospital after that suicide attempt.

In the mid-20th century, as pensions became commonplace and living standards improved, the rate of suicide among older people began a gradual decline. However in the past 15 years that trend has bottomed out, worrying groups that advocate for the aged.

"It seems that the suicide stream is running again towards an increase in rates," Professor Diego De Leo, from Griffith University, says.

In 2013, men aged 85 and over had the highest rate of suicide of any age group in Australia, according to ABS data. In the same year, if you brought the age range down to 65 and over, the number of deaths was 396—16 per cent of all suicides. (While an ageing Australia may affect the rate, the statistics do compensate for population.)

Suicide is the leading cause of death for men aged 15–19, and affects those aged 18–44 most profoundly. But what's behind a phenomenon the Council on the Ageing (CoTA) has labelled "the suicides we choose to ignore"?

"A life with too many difficulties"

It was a Wednesday in August in the Jubilee Room of the NSW State Parliament. Mr. Atkins, 67, was telling his story for a room full of medical professionals, politicians and other stakeholders, because how could he not?

For Mr. Atkins, suicide has reared its head with an almost unfathomable regularity. His first experience was in 1969, when his mother tried to kill herself in front of him. In 1987 it was his son, who even before his high school graduation had decided he was a failure in life.

"He spent three-and-a-half days in intensive care being told he'd die or be a vegetable," Mr. Atkins says.

A few years later it was Mr. Atkins' friend, Martin—a poet, novelist and son of two famous Australian writers, one of whom also happened to take her own life.

More years passed and the same story played out. Mr. Atkins lost colleagues at the CSIRO where he worked and eventually, after a combination of chronic fatigue and some bad medication he took to treat his depression, he began to think that perhaps he, too, was not fit for this world.

"There are a number of factors that have been identified," Lifeline Research Foundation executive director Alan Woodward says. "It would seem one of the key things around quality of life and happiness for older people is their perceptions around how they fit socially and with their families, how society regards them—the attitudes towards older people—and their real ability to participate in life."

Our society treats older people differently to other cultures, Mr. Woodward says. The Australian experience, unlike in many parts of Asia and the Middle East, is not one of inviting your ageing parents to live with you.

A recent Australian study, Suicide in Older Adults, found living alone was "a significant independent predictor of suicide."

Mr. Atkins tells the story of his 85-year-old uncle. "He went into a nursing home. [He and his wife] had lived together for 49-and-a-half years—they'd only been apart twice in their life, when their two sons were born. I go to visit my uncle and the first thing he says to me is 'Steve, can you help me kill myself, please? I cannot live apart from Margaret.'"

While dementia afflicts Mona Atkins, it is less prevalent, according to some research, among older people who have taken their lives than those that died in accidents or from heart attacks. That study, published in the *Journal of Psychiatric Research* in 2013, also found a lower prevalence of psychiatric problems among a group of elder suicides as compared to a group of middle aged people who also died by their own hand. The study's main conclusion: mental illness is not the whole story.

"I don't think it is very much the mental disorder but [it's] the loneliness, the impediments you have in doing many things, the difficulties in feeding yourself—the difficulties in accepting a life with too many difficulties—that may play a role," Professor De Leo says.

"So we need to embrace a holistic approach to suicide, not to narrow all attentions to mental disorders, because there is quite a number of people that don't have a mental disorder when they decide to die, particularly in old age."

Mr. Atkins also points to social exclusion as a key factor, particularly for people who had put a lot emphasis on their careers and therefore, in retirement, feel adrift. And if the stigma of men talking about their feelings remains strong anywhere, it is surely among our oldest generation.

"[They have] the feeling of incapacity to contribute to the family anymore," David Helmers, executive director of the Australian Men's Sheds Associations (AMSA), says.

He finds the high rate of suicides among men aged over 85 alarming, but not surprising. "It's a very complex problem. It's tragic. They feel worthless. If they are not seeing their families anymore, they just think, 'Why am I doing this?'"

The idea of the Men's Sheds, which operate not just around Australia but in New Zealand and the UK, is to give older men space where they can work on their own building projects and feel comfortable talking with other men about their lives.

"What we prevent is social isolation," Mr. Helmers says. "Social isolation is the tipping point. It creates poor eating, poor living, substance abuse, suicide. Lots of the key killers of men can be linked to social isolation."

"Casting out the darkness"

One day in October 2004, Noel Braun's wife, Maris, told him she was meeting up with a friend to exchange some books. Noel is pretty sure that was the only time, in 42 years of marriage, that she ever lied to him. "I sort of knew, when my wife went off," Noel, 82, says from his home in Jindabyne, at the foot of the Snowy Mountains. "I had this dreadful apprehension."

Noel and Maris had spoken of her depression, which developed 20 years earlier and seemed to get worse with age. He worked on the phones for Lifeline, so he knew the signs, and the couple were open about the topic of suicide.

Two of Maris's sisters had taken their own lives, and she had long assured Noel it would never be her fate. But in her final year, her thoughts changed.

"I knew exactly what her plan was, because I asked her," Noel says. "That was my background with Lifeline. I often told people who were completely devastated, they didn't know [about her suicidal tendencies], I said, 'Well, I did'. But I still couldn't stop her."

Maris's darkness overwhelmed her the day of her son's bucks party. She was 66. The funeral was held on the Thursday, the wedding on the Saturday. In the months afterwards, some family members invited Noel on a skiing trip to the US, and he accepted. It turned out to be a bad decision.

"When I came back it was all waiting for me, all the grief," he says. "It was sort of like a real vacuum, a real hole."

The feeling of worthlessness became oppressive, he says. He thought he had done wrong by Maris. He felt immense guilt, that he was "bad." "I reckon I was at risk myself," he says. "I was wanting to join my wife."

It was a comment from a colleague at Lifeline that turned things around, he says. "I was dwelling on all the things that I didn't do for my wife. And this lady said, 'Well, think of all the things that you did do,' and that thought really grabbed me. I did do a lot of things—it was just in those last hours, in that last day, she just slipped away. That really saved me."

He decided he wasn't going to be the strong, silent type, but would be open about the "insidious" disease of depression and his own experience with it.

Eleven years later, Noel stays active. He likes to walk. "In a way that is something that gave structure to my life, it gave me a sense of purpose," he says. "If people have a sense of purpose, it sort of makes their life meaningful."

He recently walked the Camino de Santiago pilgrimage in Spain—one month, one backpack, 700 kilometres—and he was conscious of Maris walking with him. And if the opportunity arose at the little chapels or churches he passed, he lit a candle for her. The candle has great symbolic meaning, he says: "It's casting out the darkness."

"It's an Epidemic"

As for what can be done to decrease the number of older people taking their lives, many experts say the problem is complex.

But Mr. Woodward says Australia could do better in having suicide prevention techniques integrated into the aged care system. He points to the US where he says guides on suicide prevention are distributed in aged care homes, with the stress of relocation noted as a factor in suicidal tendencies.

Family support can also be a very significant "protective factor," he says. "Families [can] directly address the issue of isolation, so that an older person, perhaps living alone, can still participate in family visits and activities and have a sense of meaning and purpose within that family."

Meanwhile, Mr. Helmers says that changes to access to unemployment benefits for older Australians may have a positive effect.

He uses the example of a man who spent his life installing right-side car doors at a Ford factory but was laid off at 55.

"From a commercial sense, his prospects are quite minimal," he says. And yet he must fulfil the same job search and training requirements as someone applying for the dole at 18. A relaxing of those standards, Mr. Helmers says, might make entry back into the workforce easier, something that is particularly important given the retirement age will rise to 67 by 2023.

Of course, while groups such as CoTA and AMSA advocate for greater awareness of the suicides among older Australians—and therefore greater resourcing—it is important to put the issue into perspective. In 2013, men aged 85 and over had the highest suicide rate—38 deaths per 100,000 people—but as a proportion of total male deaths among this age group, suicide accounted for less than 1 per cent. In contrast, for men aged 40-44—the group with the second-highest suicide death rate—17 per cent of deaths were the result of suicide. For men aged 15 to 19—the age group at which so much suicide prevention work is directed—the figures are even worse. One in three deaths are the result of suicide.

Mr. Helmers argues there does need to be a reallocation of resources, citing unpublished Victorian Coroners Court data he says shows the majority of the state's 2,200 suicides in a recent year were of men aged over 45.

"It's logical, isn't it? If that's where the numbers are, that's where the money should be going," he says. "Youth suicides are tragic, but with older people it's an epidemic."

Mr. Woodward points to a similar issue: that as a society we don't look at the older life as any less valuable than the younger when it comes to suicide prevention.

"Certainly, we need to put much more money and efforts into suicide [prevention] in a coordinated manner," Professor De Leo says. "We need to invest much more in research. We need to create many tailored—by age and gender—programs and evaluate them carefully, which is something that we weren't too good in doing so far.

"However, I believe we are doing still too little to have a significant government impact on suicides, and we are doing even less for the elderly because we continue to consider the elderly as less important than young people."

> *"The common thread for all these issues is the need to safeguard the dignity, autonomy and self-determination in care and treatment choices for older persons, given the specificities of their human rights situation."*

The Elderly Deserve Dignity and Autonomy in Care

Nils Muižnieks

In the following viewpoint, Nils Muižnieks argues that aging brings with it myriad problems, and European nations must be proactive to anticipate a populace that is growing older. While many older adults are able to defy common aging stereotypes, there are numerous others who do require substantial care, and it is up to nations to provide this care. As much as possible, it is advantageous to allow the elderly to live independent lives, but if care is required, it should be given in a manner that respects the personhood of each individual. Nils Muižnieks is a Latvian-American human rights activist who serves as commissioner for human rights for the Council of Europe.

"The Right of Older Persons to Dignity and Autonomy in Care," by Nils Muižnieks, Council of Europe, January 18, 2018. Reprinted by permission.

As you read, consider the following questions:

1. What specific problems often affect older people?
2. What steps do European nations need to take to account for an aging population?
3. What problems ensue when professionals underestimate the degree of pain a patient is suffering from?

Older persons have exactly the same rights as everyone else, but when it comes to the implementation of these rights, they face a number of specific challenges. For example, they often face age discrimination, particular forms of social exclusion, economic marginalisation due to inadequate pensions, or are more vulnerable to exploitation and abuse, including from family members.

These challenges require specific policy responses in the context of a rapidly ageing world population, but particularly so in Europe which already has the highest median age in the world: the World Health Organisation (WHO) estimates that 25% of Europeans will be aged 65 and older by 2050 (from 14% in 2010). Against this background, the question of the human rights of older persons has been receiving more attention within the UN system, but also the Council of Europe, for example in the form of a Recommendation by the Committee of Ministers on the promotion of human rights of older persons adopted in 2014.

We need to acknowledge that the existence of many stereotypes about older persons as being helpless, in poor health or dependent could be a problem in itself and that it is not uncommon for older persons to defy these stereotypes: Claudio Arrau, one of the greatest concert pianists of the 20th century, continued touring, recording and extending his repertoire well into his 80s. However, it is also a reality that many of us must face increasing frailty as a natural consequence of the ageing process, sometimes together with cognitive impairment, reducing the independence that we crave and increasing the need for care. When this need is such that help is required for daily tasks, such as shopping, cooking, eating, cleaning or bathing, over a long period of time, we speak of a need for long-term care.

Long-Term Care

The European Social Charter, the point of reference for social rights in Europe, was the first international convention to provide specifically for care for older persons. States who have accepted Article 23 of the Revised Social Charter (or Article 4 of the 1988 Additional Protocol to the 1961 Charter) have the obligation to enable older persons to remain full members of society for as long as possible. This includes enabling them to lead independent lives in their familiar surroundings as long as they wish and are able, by adapting their housing to their state of health and by providing the health care and the services they need. For older persons living in residential institutions, states must guarantee appropriate support, while respecting privacy, and participation in decisions concerning their living conditions. Unfortunately, only 20 member states have accepted this provision to date.

As recognised by the Parliamentary Assembly of the Council of Europe (PACE) in May 2017 in a Resolution devoted to the question of the human rights of older persons and their comprehensive care, the access of older persons to good quality health care and long-term care remains a challenge in Europe.

The European Network of National Human Rights Institutions (ENNHRI) has been conducting a very valuable project on the human rights of older persons in long-term care since 2015. In June 2017, it published a report which took as its basis the monitoring work carried out by six of its members (the National Human Rights Institutions in Belgium, Croatia, Germany, Hungary, Lithuania and Romania). The report shows that, in spite of good practices and the hard work and dedication of many care workers, human rights concerns were found in care homes in all six countries (mirroring similar research carried out by 11 other ENNHRI members in recent years), notably due to a lack of resources and the failure to

Human Rights and the Elderly

In recent years, there have been significant advocacy efforts calling for enhanced international thinking and action on the human rights of older persons. Various stakeholders have called for more visibility and increased use of international human rights standards to address the dire situation of millions of older women and men around the world.

Not very long ago, the issue of ageing was considered a matter of importance for only a handful of countries. Nowadays, the number of persons aged 60 and over is increasing at an unprecedented pace, anticipated to rise from its current 740 million to reach 1 billion by the end of the decade. Unfortunately the increase in numbers has also shed light on the lack of adequate protection mechanisms, and on the existing gaps in policies and programmes to address the situation of older persons. Today, two-thirds of the world's older people live in low- and middle-income countries and this proportion will rise to 80 per cent by 2050.

Older persons are not a homogenous group, and the challenges they face in the protection or enjoyment of their human rights vary greatly. While some continue to lead active lives as part of their community, many others face homelessness, lack of adequate care or isolation.

use a human rights–based approach in the design and delivery of long-term care.

Of course long-term care is not limited to residential settings and persons requiring it should be offered the possibility to choose their living arrangements, with adequate supports. Of particular relevance in this respect is the United Nations Convention on the Rights of Persons with Disabilities (CRPD), ratified by 45 of the 47 member states of the Council of Europe and by the EU: in addition to its Article 25 on Health which acknowledges the needs of older persons, the CRPD also provides for the right to live independently and to be included in the community in its Article 19. This right, along with dignity and self-determination, must be guiding principles for the design of long-term care

Multiple discrimination appears as an essential component of any analysis, particularly when considering that age-related discrimination if often compounded by other grounds of discrimination, such as sex, socio-economic status, ethnicity, or health status.

The Office of the High Commissioner for Human Rights strives to ensure that neglected population groups are given space and weight in the human rights agenda, and that governments take all measures required to protect and promote their human rights. The role of the Office is to ensure a voice for all, especially for those whose voices are seldom heard.

For the first time the Report of the Secretary-General to the General Assembly focuses on the human rights of older persons. It identifies four main challenges older persons are facing in terms of human rights as discrimination, poverty, violence and abuse as well as the lack of specific measures and services. The report further stresses several key areas for responses to the challenges as strengthening the international protection regime, elimination of financial exploitation and employment discrimination, establishing adequate care facilities and participation in political life.

"Human Rights of Older Persons," Office of the High Commissioner for Human Rights.

services, including in residential settings, where the majority of care recipients are estimated to have a form of disability.

Very worryingly, research and analyses of national policy reforms indicate that, despite the urgency of rethinking long-term care in the context of the rapidly growing ageing population of Europe, many Member States are not adequately planning for these future challenges, but are instead improvising, with short-term fixes. This is likely to further aggravate already existing problems of access to long-term care, which can sometimes be available only to those with the highest care needs or those who can afford to pay for them, as well as compromising the quality of services and the protection of the human rights and dignity of their recipients.

It is recognised that older persons are highly vulnerable to abuse, including in long-term care, the WHO estimating that at least 4 million older persons experience maltreatment in the European region every year. In a case concerning a geriatric nurse who was dismissed for having brought a criminal case against her employer alleging deficiencies in the care provided (*Heinisch v. Germany*, 21 July 2011), the European Court of Human Rights recognised this problem, stating that "in societies with an ever growing part of their elderly population being subject to institutional care, and taking into account the particular vulnerability of the patients concerned, who often may not be in a position to draw attention to shortcomings in the provision of care on their own initiative, the dissemination of information about the quality or deficiencies of such care is of vital importance with a view to preventing abuse."

In this context, while the ENNHRI members collaborating for the above mentioned report did not find evidence of outright torture or deliberate abuse as such, worrying practices were detected in all six countries, raising serious concerns about upholding dignity, the right to privacy, autonomy, participation, and access to justice. These included, among many other examples, verbal and physical aggression; lack of adequate medical care, as well as overuse of medication; locking doors from the outside; disrespecting the intimacy of residents, for example, by bathing them at the same time; lack of heating or insufficient food to save money; or preventing residents from making complaints. It is not excluded that some of these occurrences of neglect could potentially be serious enough as to constitute a violation of Article 3 of the ECHR (prohibition of inhuman or degrading treatment).

It is urgent for member states to thoroughly review, with the participation of older persons, their approach to long-term care in order to make it more human rights–based, including in the light of the Revised Social Charter (by accepting Article 23 if they have not yet done so), the 2014 Recommendation of the Committee of Ministers, and the 2017 Resolution of the PACE. In addition to providing the resources such a system requires to be accessible and affordable, states must also take account of the training needs of care professionals, as well as of informal caregivers, and ensure that the choices for older persons are maximised, for example when they wish to live in their home, while preventing social isolation (the 2003 heat wave in France which killed many older persons was a terrible wake-up call about the risks of such isolation). Particular attention should be paid to ensure regular independent monitoring of long-term care services on the basis of clear principles and rights that older persons can easily enforce themselves. I encourage member states and care givers to make full use in this process of the relevant toolkit of ENNHRI.

Palliative Care

Another important aspect of the right of older persons to dignity and autonomy in care concerns palliative care. Palliative care is an approach that improves the quality of life of patients and their families facing life-limiting illness, mainly through pain and symptom relief, but also through psychosocial support. This is contrasted with curative medicine, for which the goals of curing an illness or extending the patient's life come before the subjective well-being of the patient. However, palliative care and curative treatment can be administered in parallel.

While palliative care concerns persons of all ages suffering from life-limiting illnesses, such as cancer, lack of specific measures to avoid pain or to allow the terminally ill to die with dignity naturally affects older persons in a disproportionate manner, as they experience increased rates of chronic and terminal illnesses involving moderate to severe pain. This is again of concern in the European region given the projected demographic developments.

The importance of palliative care as an integral part of health services and its denial as a human rights violation are being increasingly recognised at the international level. Special Rapporteurs of the UN on Torture and on Health stated that the denial of pain relief causing severe pain and suffering may amount to cruel, inhuman or degrading treatment. Within the Council of

Europe, the above mentioned Recommendation of the Committee of Ministers on the human rights of older persons devoted a chapter to palliative care, providing that "any older person who is in need of palliative care should be entitled to access it without undue delay, in a setting which is consistent with his or her needs and preferences, including at home and in long-term care settings."

However access to palliative care and pain relief remains problematic. Human Rights Watch reports that many countries in Europe are affected by shortcomings regarding palliative care, such as the lack of a palliative care policy and of pain management training of carers, as well as problems of regulation and availability of opioids. I was heartened to see that Armenia and Ukraine, where these problems caused extremely intense, needless suffering until very recently, are now making progress in the right direction. However many other countries continue to face similar problems.

When it comes to older persons more specifically, a WHO report underlined how pain is frequently underassessed for older people, in particular for persons with dementia, and pointed to a widespread failure to inform and involve patients in decision-making, lack of home care, of access to specialist services and of palliative care within residential homes. A deficient palliative care policy also leads to frequent cases where older people undergo unnecessary examinations, treatments, hospitalisations and admissions to intensive care, sometimes against their own will. This is burdensome and expensive for the patient, family and society. All member states need to have a serious rethink of their palliative care policy to address such shortcomings.

An issue that is relevant in this connection is "advance directives" or "living wills," i.e. documents which allow one to freely express one's will, for example as regards care planning, so that it can be respected when one is no longer in a position to express it oneself, due to the loss of consciousness or ability to make decisions. These documents are particularly relevant for older persons with degenerative illnesses, such as Alzheimer's disease. Their value has been repeatedly recognised by the Council of

Europe, but practice is extremely variable among member states. I welcome the debate that took place on this question recently in Italy, culminating in the adoption of the so-called Biotestamento Law, but such debate is necessary in many other member states.

The common thread for all these issues is the need to safeguard the dignity, autonomy and self-determination in care and treatment choices for older persons, given the specificities of their human rights situation. Many argue that this situation points to a need for a binding international legal instrument, and I am happy to note the on-going work within the UN to assess this need. I also fully endorse the recent call of the PACE for a similar assessment, with the involvement of older persons, within the Council of Europe.

Periodical and Internet Sources Bibliography

The following articles have been selected to supplement the diverse views presented in this chapter.

Jonathan Arena, "Life a Path, Death a Destination," Georgia Right to Life. http://www.grtl.org/?q=life-a-path-death-a-destination

Brian Clowes, "Shouldn't Women Be Able to Control Their Own Bodies?" Human Life International, May 27, 2018. https://www .hli.org/resources/shouldnt-women-able-control-bodies

Evelyn French, "Seven Suggestions for Recognizing the Personhood of the Preborn," *Celebrate Life Magazine*, Winter 2018. https:// www.clmagazine.org/topic/human-dignity/seven-suggestions -for-recognizing-the-personhood-of-the-preborn/

Jeannie Suk Gerson, "How Fetal Personhood Emerged as the Next Stage of the Abortion Wars," *New Yorker*, June 5, 2019. https:// www.newyorker.com/news/our-columnists/how-fetal -personhood-emerged-as-the-next-stage-of-the-abortion-wars

Douglas O. Linder, "The Other Right-to-Life Debate: When Does Fourteenth Amendment 'Life' End?" *Arizona Law Review*, Winter 1995. http://law2.umkc.edu/faculty/projects/ftrials/conlaw /Lifedebate.html

Georgina Nelson, "Maintaining the Integrity of Personhood in Palliative Care," *Scottish Journal of Healthcare Chaplaincy,* Vol. 3. No. 2, 2000. https://citeseerx.ist.psu.edu/viewdoc /download?doi=10.1.1.538.6627&rep=rep1&type=pdf

Dónal P. O'Mathúna, "Personhood in Bioethics and Biomedical Research," *Research Practitioner*, Vol. 7, No. 5, Sept.–Oct. 2006. https://www.scribd.com/document/410219485/RP-Personhood -SeptOct2006-pdf

David Orentlicher, "Abortion and the Fetal Personhood Fallacy," Bill of Health, August 11, 2015. https://blog.petrieflom.law.harvard .edu/2015/08/11/abortion-and-the-fetal-personhood-fallacy/

Katha Pollitt, "Fetal Personhood Is Maternal Punishment," *The Nation*, December 16/23, 2019. https://www.thenation.com /article/archive/abortion-csection-birth/

Abe Sauer, "The Unintended Consequences of Personhood," Reuters, November 9, 2011. https://www.reuters.com/article/idUS423114743920111109

Jillian A. Tullis, "Personhood and Communication at the End of Life," *Journal of Medicine and the Person*, 10, pp. 103–113, 2012. https://link.springer.com/article/10.1007/s12682-012-0131-0

Could Artificial Intelligence Attain Personhood?

Chapter Preface

Artificial intelligence (AI) personhood may be a relatively new concept in the real world, but science fiction writers have been kicking it around for many years. The plot of Philip K. Dick's 1968 novel *Do Androids Dream of Electric Sheep?* and the film that was based on it, *Blade Runner,* revolve around humanoids who are able to pass for real human beings. Rick Deckard is the police officer/blade runner tasked with "retiring" (killing) these androids against their will. In his 1942 short story "Runaround," which appeared in the volume *I, Robot*, Isaac Asimov famously listed three rules for artificial humans:

> First Law: A robot may not injure a human being or, through inaction, allow a human being to come to harm.
>
> Second Law: A robot must obey the orders given it by human beings except where such orders would conflict with the First Law.
>
> Third Law: A robot must protect its own existence as long as such protection does not conflict with the First or Second Law.

In the late twentieth and early twenty-first centuries, some of Asimov's concerns have become reality. In particular, debate has erupted over exactly who is at fault if an artificially intelligent "being" causes harm to humans. AI personhood has become a controversial answer to the question. "In a resolution of 2017, the European Parliament urged the European Commission to propose what it called 'electronic personality' for sophisticated autonomous robots," writes Thomas Burri, assistant professor of international law and European law at the University of St. Gallen in Switzerland. Such a law, if enacted, would absolve corporations that manufacture robots and other AI and make the artificial being the sole defendant if and when it went haywire and caused harm to humans or property.

But how does one sue a robot, which, of course, has no assets beyond itself? In April 2018, a group of experts in the field of AI published an open letter urging the European Commission to reject giving such protection to corporations. "From an ethical and legal perspective, creating a legal personality for a robot is inappropriate," they wrote.

While it is clear that laws worldwide must be enacted to account for the actions of artificially intelligent beings, the exact nature of such laws is still undecided. As Philip K. Dick and Isaac Asimov correctly intuited, there were many more grey concepts in connection with artificially intelligent beings than there were black and white ones.

Artificial intelligence currently depends on the computer algorithms that software engineers program into them. Thus, science is a long way from creating artificial beings that can think or feel emotions. Even so, programmers are creating AI that can delve into the arts, which are often viewed as more expressive and emotional that other disciplines. For example, programmers are "enabling computers to make up original fugues in the style of Bach, improvise jazz solos à la John Coltrane, or mash up the two into a hybrid never heard before."[1] It is one thing to enable a Roomba to vacuum floors. It is another step entirely up the robot evolutionary scale to have them dabble in the arts.

While the overwhelming majority of those in the field of AI would admit that we are still a long way off from creating truly sentient artificial beings—those that display self-awareness—there is still an acknowledgement that AI will come closer and closer to this goal. What becomes clear is that governments must start planning for the inevitable creation of increasingly sophisticated robots, androids, and other artificial intelligence.

Endnotes

1. William Hockberg, "When Robots Write Songs." *Atlantic*. August 7, 2014.
   https://www.theatlantic.com/entertainment/archive/2014/08/computers
   -that-compose/374916/

> *"If AI systems became more intelligent than people, humans could be relegated to an inferior role—as workers hired and fired by AI corporate overlords—or even challenged for social dominance."*

Granting Personhood to Artificial Intelligence Is Dangerous

Roman V. Yampolskiy

In the following viewpoint, Roman V. Yampolskiy discusses how legal loopholes could be used to grant artificial intelligence the same rights as humans. The author cites a specific example of how, under the current laws that grant personhood to corporations, robots could also be given human rights. But, Yampolskiy argues, such a development is dangerous. The proliferation of artificial intelligence with rights equal to humans could affect voting, drive corporate greed, and lead to a world dominated by computers instead of people. Roman V. Yampolskiy is associate professor in the Department of Computer Engineering and Computer Science at the University of Louisville.

As you read, consider the following questions:

1. How, under current law, might personhood be given to AI?
2. How is Saudi law already problematic for women's rights?
3. What problems might arrive with regard to voting if AI is given personhood status?

Humans aren't the only people in society—at least according to the law. In the US, corporations have been given rights of free speech and religion. Some natural features also have person-like rights. But both of those required changes to the legal system. A new argument has laid a path for artificial intelligence systems to be recognized as people too—without any legislation, court rulings or other revisions to existing law.

Legal scholar Shawn Bayern has shown that anyone can confer legal personhood on a computer system, by putting it in control of a limited liability corporation in the US. If that maneuver is upheld in courts, artificial intelligence systems would be able to own property, sue, hire lawyers and enjoy freedom of speech and other protections under the law. In my view, human rights and dignity would suffer as a result.

The Corporate Loophole

Giving AIs rights similar to humans involves a technical lawyerly maneuver. It starts with one person setting up two limited liability companies and turning over control of each company to a separate autonomous or artificially intelligent system. Then the person would add each company as a member of the other LLC. In the last step, the person would withdraw from both LLCs, leaving each LLC—a corporate entity with legal personhood—governed only by the other's AI system.

That process doesn't require the computer system to have any particular level of intelligence or capability. It could just be a sequence of "if" statements looking, for example, at the stock market and making decisions to buy and sell based on prices falling or rising. It could even be an algorithm that makes decisions randomly, or an emulation of an amoeba.

Reducing Human Status

Granting human rights to a computer would degrade human dignity. For instance, when Saudi Arabia granted citizenship to a robot called Sophia, human women, including feminist scholars, objected, noting that the robot was given more rights than many Saudi women have.

In certain places, some people might have fewer rights than nonintelligent software and robots. In countries that limit citizens' rights to free speech, free religious practice and expression of sexuality, corporations—potentially including AI-run companies— could have more rights. That would be an enormous indignity.

The risk doesn't end there: If AI systems became more intelligent than people, humans could be relegated to an inferior role—as workers hired and fired by AI corporate overlords—or even challenged for social dominance.

Artificial intelligence systems could be tasked with law enforcement among human populations—acting as judges, jurors, jailers and even executioners. Warrior robots could similarly be assigned to the military and given power to decide on targets and acceptable collateral damage—even in violation of international humanitarian laws. Most legal systems are not set up to punish robots or otherwise hold them accountable for wrongdoing.

What About Voting?

Granting voting rights to systems that can copy themselves would render humans' votes meaningless. Even without taking that significant step, though, the possibility of AI-controlled corporations with basic human rights poses serious dangers. No current laws would prevent a malevolent AI from operating a corporation that worked to subjugate or exterminate humanity through legal means and political influence. Computer-controlled companies could turn out to be less responsive to public opinion or protests than human-run firms are.

Immortal Wealth

Two other aspects of corporations make people even more vulnerable to AI systems with human legal rights: They don't die, and they can give unlimited amounts of money to political candidates and groups.

Artificial intelligences could earn money by exploiting workers, using algorithms to price goods and manage investments, and find new ways to automate key business processes. Over long periods of time, that could add up to enormous earnings—which would never be split up among descendants. That wealth could easily be converted into political power.

Politicians financially backed by algorithmic entities would be able to take on legislative bodies, impeach presidents and help to get figureheads appointed to the Supreme Court. Those human figureheads could be used to expand corporate rights or even establish new rights specific to artificial intelligence systems—expanding the threats to humanity even more.

> *"By adopting legal personhood, we are going to erase the responsibility of manufacturers."*

Robot Personhood Is a Divisive Issue

Janosch Delcker

In the following viewpoint, Janosch Delcker argues that robots can be insured individually, like people, and then held accountable for any damages should they run amok. On the other hand, robot personhood is a slippery slope toward granting artificial intelligence the same rights as humans. If personhood is granted to robots, manufacturers are absolved from facing the consequences of their actions. With production of artificially intelligent beings exploding, the issue of robot personhood will only become more important. Janosch Delcker is an award-winning political journalist based in Berlin, Germany. He has published feature stories, radio pieces, and TV documentaries for Politico, *the* New York Times, *the* Intercept, *and numerous other publications.*

As you read, consider the following questions:

1. What is an "electronic personality"?
2. How will advances in robot technology make litigation even more difficult?
3. How close are scientists, currently, to creating truly sentient machines that can behave like humans?

Think lawsuits involving humans are tricky? Try taking an intelligent robot to court.

While autonomous robots with humanlike, all-encompassing capabilities are still decades away, European lawmakers, legal experts and manufacturers are already locked in a high-stakes debate about their legal status: whether it's these machines or human beings who should bear ultimate responsibility for their actions.

The battle goes back to a paragraph of text, buried deep in a European Parliament report from early 2017, which suggests that self-learning robots could be granted "electronic personalities." Such a status could allow robots to be insured individually and be held liable for damages if they go rogue and start hurting people or damaging property.

Those pushing for such a legal change, including some manufacturers and their affiliates, say the proposal is common sense. Legal personhood would not make robots virtual people who can get married and benefit from human rights, they say; it would merely put them on par with corporations, which already have status as "legal persons," and are treated as such by courts around the world.

But as robots and artificial intelligence become hot-button political issues on both sides of the Atlantic, MEP and vice chair of the European Parliament's legal affairs committee, Mady Delvaux, and other proponents of legal changes face stiffening opposition. In a letter to the European Commission seen by POLITICO and expected to be unveiled Thursday, 156 artificial intelligence experts hailing from 14 European countries, including computer scientists, law professors and CEOs, warn that granting robots legal personhood would be "inappropriate" from a "legal and ethical perspective."

The report from the Parliament's legal affairs committee recommended the idea of giving robots "electronic personalities," and could become a model for laws across Europe if turned into regulatory framework. Delvaux said that while she was not sure that legally defining robots as personalities was a good idea, she was "more and more convinced" that current legislation was insufficient to deal with complex issues surrounding liability and self-learning machines and that all options should be put on the table.

The AI experts behind the letter to the European Commission strongly disagree.

"By adopting legal personhood, we are going to erase the responsibility of manufacturers," said Nathalie Navejans, a French law professor at the Université d'Artois, who was the driving force behind the letter.

Noel Sharkey, emeritus professor of artificial intelligence and robotics at the University of Sheffield, who also signed on, added that by seeking legal personhood for robots, manufacturers were merely trying to absolve themselves of responsibility for the actions of their machines.

"This [European Parliament position] was what I'd call a slimy way of manufacturers getting out of their responsibility," he said.

"Black Box" Robots

As each side turns up the volume on its advocacy, one thing is clear: Money is pouring into the field of robotics, and the debate is set to turn louder.

In coming years, analysts predict the gold rush into emerging fields is only set to accelerate. The market for consumer robots, for instance—machines acting as companions in the household—is expected to almost triple within the next five years, from $5.4 billion in 2018 to $14.9 billion by 2023.

Sales of "cobots"—machines designed to work alongside humans—are forecast as increasing almost thirtyfold, from just over $100 million in 2015 to $3 billion in 2020.

And the market for industrial robots—machines that can, for example, put together cars or perform sophisticated assembly line tasks—is expected to balloon as well, reaching $40 billion by 2020, compared to $25.7 billion in 2013.

The current boom has to do with the fact that robots just entered the second stage of their evolution, 59 years after the first industrial robot joined the assembly line of American General Motors factories.

In the decades that followed, machines remained largely reactive, programmed to complete defined tasks and react to a limited number of situations.

The latest developments, by contrast, enable machines to fulfill tasks that previously required human thinking. Current state-of-the-art technology allows computers to learn and make their own decisions by mimicking and proliferating human brain patterns.

The concern of lawmakers: Will such complex processes turn machines into "black boxes" whose decision-making processes are difficult or even impossible to understand, and therefore impenetrable for litigators seeking to attribute legal responsibility for problems?

Can Robots Marry?

That's why, advocates argue, Europe should grant "legal status" to the robots themselves, rather than burden their manufacturers or owners.

"In a scenario where an algorithm can take autonomous decision, then who should be responsible for these decisions?" Milan-based corporate lawyer Stefania Lucchetti said.

The current model, in which either the manufacturer, the owner, or both are liable, would become defunct in an age of fully autonomous robots, and the EU should give robots some sort of legal personality "like companies have," she added.

The "personality" she referred to is a concept that dates back to the 13th century, when Pope Innocent IV granted personhood status to monasteries. Today, virtually every country of the world applies the model to companies, which means that corporations have some of the legal rights and responsibilities of a human being, including being able to sign a contract or being sued. A similar legal model for robots, its advocates argue, would be less about giving rights to robots and rather about holding them responsible when things go wrong, for example by setting up a compulsory insurance scheme that could be fed by the wealth a robot is accumulating over the time of its "existence."

"This doesn't mean the robot is self-conscious, or can marry another robot," Lucchetti said.

Along similar lines, Delvaux stressed that the idea behind coming up with an electronic personality was not about giving human rights to robots—but to make sure that a robot is and will remain a machine with a human backing it.

Beyond Sophia

The controversy swirling around futuristic robots masks the reality that robots capable of human-like intelligence and decision-making remain a far-off prospect.

Today's robots are better than humans at some narrow applications, such as recognizing images, or playing the Chinese board game Go.

But such state-of-the-art applications excel only in one narrow field. Playing Go, or categorizing images, are essentially the only things such machines can do, unlike human beings, who can at the same time understand language, learn to play a variety of board games and recognize images.

Even so, media reports about galloping advances in robotics—which may suggest all-encompassing robot intelligence is within reach—have infiltrated public debate. That may lead lawmakers to rush into premature regulation, the signatories of the letter warn.

According to some researchers, no robot has done as much to convey false notions about robotics as Sophia: a humanoid robot that made its first appearance in March 2016 and has since then become a Saudi Arabian citizen, was given a title from the United Nations and opened the Munich Security Conference this year.

"I don't mind the idea of a show robot at all," said Sharkey, who co-signed the letter and is also co-founder of the Foundation for Responsible Robotics. "But when they start bringing it to the U.N. and giving nations the wrong idea of what robotics can do and where AI is at the moment it's very, very dangerous."

He added: "It's very dangerous for lawmakers as well. They see this and they believe it, because they're not engineers and there is no reason not to believe it."

Instead, the EU's existing civil law rules are sufficient to address questions of liability, the 156 AI experts argue in their open letter.

Delvaux said the Parliament's discussion about a full electronic personality is ongoing, and that "maybe at the end of the day, we'll come to the conclusion that it is not a good idea."

Her primary goal when suggesting legal personhood for robots was to raise a public debate about the issue, she said.

In that sense, she succeeded.

"*Artificial intelligence is meant to be a tool for humans, to make our lives easier and find solutions to everyday problems. It is not meant to replace us. And yet, we design it to replicate human-ness with eerie fidelity.*"

Human-Like AI Is Dangerous to Society

Kat Mustatea

In the following viewpoint, Kat Mustatea discusses the propensity for making artificial intelligence as human as possible and the reasons why manufacturers do so. Even though AI is meant to serve humans and make its owner's life easier, creators are making it as realistic as possible, to the point where the line between humans and machines is sometimes blurred. The idea, Mustatea writes, is that humans respond to creations that mimic their own actions. Ultimately, Mustatea wonders, will humans control AI or be controlled by it? Kat Mustatea is an artist and technologist whose recent TED talk examines the meaning of machines making art.

"Human-Like AI Is Dangerous for Society," by Kat Mustatea, The Week Publications Inc., August 8, 2018. Reprinted by permission.

As you read, consider the following questions:

1. Why do manufacturers make anthropomorphized machines?
2. What does the viewpoint find disturbing about Saudi Arabia's "granting citizenship" to a talking robot?
3. What example does the author offer as a way to involve non-technical people in the design of systems that affect their lives?

The voice on the other end of the phone sounded just a little too human.

In May, Google shocked the world with a demo of Duplex, its AI robocall assistant for accomplishing real-world tasks. The system can do things that you, as a busy person, might have little time or patience for, like booking a hair appointment or a restaurant reservation. But with its authentic-sounding "hmms" and "uhs," the system raised some serious concerns, because the humans who answered the phone calls did not seem to realize they were talking to a piece of software. And indeed, this should worry us. Convincing human-like AI could be deployed for dubious reasons with disastrous consequences.

As more and more people come in contact with autonomous systems like Duplex, the danger is not that these systems will suddenly wake up and take over the world, despite the hysterical portrayals in the media and pop culture. Instead, the real danger is that humans will become but a passive data point in the designing of those systems, to disastrous ends.

Artificial intelligence is meant to be a tool for humans, to make our lives easier and find solutions to everyday problems. It is not meant to replace us. And yet, we design it to replicate human-ness with eerie fidelity. We don't do this with other tools—hammers look like hammers, not people—so why do we do this with AI?

The answer is simple: because it makes great marketing.

When machines accommodate and gesture toward the nuances of our own behavior, we are much more willing to integrate them into our lives. Things that look and sound like us trigger our admirable human capacity for empathy. In the case of Duplex, the closer a voice sounds to human, the more reluctant the receiver of a robocall might be to hang up. But the human-ness of artificial intelligence could easily mask a dubious attempt to sell you something. Indeed, it could become all too easy to commoditize our trust. For example, we might be prone to read friendly intent into a bank chatbot that makes warm and witty banter, even if its purpose is to push students toward taking out unnecessary loans.

There are other concerning examples of AI being anthropomorphized and used as a marketing ploy. Last October, Saudi Arabia made headlines by "granting citizenship" to a talking robot named Sophia. This was a marketing stunt meant to signal the country's focus on technological innovation. But if we look more closely, this move should be considered especially cruel in a country that only allowed real human women to drive last year, and where women still require a male guardian to make financial and legal decisions. A robot, it seems, can breezily be granted more rights than half of the population of that country, all for a short-term spot in the news cycle.

Perhaps this seems like an overreaction. But I assure you, it is not. Talk of AI and personhood at the level of nations, even if it starts as a marketing stunt, can have far-reaching repercussions. A proposal now before the European Union would grant robots a distinct status of "electronic persons," a move that attempts to answer the question of who is to blame when AI behavior has lethal consequences. "The more autonomous robots are, the less they can be considered simple tools in the hands of other actors (such as the manufacturer, the owner, the user, etc.)," the proposal reads: "This, in turn, makes the ordinary rules on liability insufficient and calls for new rules which focus on how a machine can be held—partly or entirely—responsible for its acts or omissions."

This kind of language, if enacted, is a disastrous misappropriation of human responsibility. When we are unwilling to hold humans accountable for the systems they create and release into the world, and instead allow an "electronic person" to bear the blame, we are no better than children who point the finger at an invisible "friend" for the bowl they themselves have broken. The resulting laws warp people's notion of AI in ways that make society less free, and less able to benefit from the cutting edge technologies that are within our reach.

"Pull back the curtain of AI and there are millions of exploited people," writes the technology pioneer Jaron Lanier in his book, *Dawn of the New Everything*: "The only way to reduce the harm is to stop believing in AI as a new type of creature, but instead evaluate algorithms as tools to be used by people."

It is time to think more critically about the impact of anthropomorphizing software. The first step is to see anthropomorphized AI for the marketing ploy it is. But the real antidote is to actively look for ways non-technical people can be involved in the design of the systems that affect their lives.

One recent project at Columbia University's Gang Intervention and Computer Science Project provides an example of how this might be done. William Frey and his colleagues describe how formerly gang-involved young people in Chicago were hired as subject matter experts in the development of a system to monitor and prevent gang violence. Such monitoring systems for social media are already used by police—but without the important context and nuance former members of those communities provide, the systems can be wrong and innocent people can be arrested and criminalized based on little more than a tweet.

While a number of big companies have launched internal programs to implement ethical guardrails around the use of AI, these remain largely opaque processes enacted at the executive levels of private corporations. As for Google's Duplex, a second demo in June was explicit in highlighting ways the system might disclose its status as a machine at the outset of a robocall.

Still, a good question to ask of software made to mimic us is: What aspect of the human is being imitated, and to what end? Does the specific product or system have to be anthropomorphic in its design to be effective? How we answer this question could have broad implications for how we interact with AI in the future. We can move through the digital age in deference to our robotic overlords, or we might be savvy enough to realize we are the ones in charge.

> *"By inventing revolutionary new technologies, such a superintelligence might help us eradicate war, disease, and poverty, and so the creation of strong AI might be the biggest event in human history."*

We Must Align the Goals of AI with Ours Before It Goes Too Far

Max Tegmark

In the following viewpoint, Max Tegmark argues that while artificial intelligence exists to aid humans, the creation of super intelligent AI that can outperform humans in all cognitive tasks poses a great risk. As scientists are in uncharted territory when it comes to creating what he calls "strong AI," it is hard to determine just how to keep AI under human control. As machines grow increasingly competent, scientists must keep the goals of AI in line with humanity's goals. Max Tegmark is a physicist, cosmologist, and machine learning researcher. He is a professor at the Massachusetts Institute of Technology and the scientific director of the Foundational Questions Institute.

"Benefits & Risks of Artificial Intelligence," by Max Tegmark, FLI — Future of Life Institute. Reprinted by permission.

As you read, consider the following questions:

1. How does the author distinguish between weak AI and strong AI?
2. What are two specific scenarios where Tegmark believes AI can get out of hand?
3. What is the prevailing wisdom among scientists about how long it will take to create superhuman AI?

From SIRI to self-driving cars, artificial intelligence (AI) is progressing rapidly. While science fiction often portrays AI as robots with human-like characteristics, AI can encompass anything from Google's search algorithms to IBM's Watson to autonomous weapons.

Artificial intelligence today is properly known as narrow AI (or weak AI), in that it is designed to perform a narrow task (e.g. only facial recognition or only internet searches or only driving a car). However, the long-term goal of many researchers is to create general AI (AGI or strong AI). While narrow AI may outperform humans at whatever its specific task is, like playing chess or solving equations, AGI would outperform humans at nearly every cognitive task.

Why Research AI Safety?

In the near term, the goal of keeping AI's impact on society beneficial motivates research in many areas, from economics and law to technical topics such as verification, validity, security and control. Whereas it may be little more than a minor nuisance if your laptop crashes or gets hacked, it becomes all the more important that an AI system does what you want it to do if it controls your car, your airplane, your pacemaker, your automated trading system or your power grid. Another short-term challenge is preventing a devastating arms race in lethal autonomous weapons.

In the long term, an important question is what will happen if the quest for strong AI succeeds and an AI system becomes better than humans at all cognitive tasks. As pointed out by I.J. Good in 1965, designing smarter AI systems is itself a cognitive task. Such a system could potentially undergo recursive self-improvement, triggering an intelligence explosion leaving human intellect far behind. By inventing revolutionary new technologies, such a superintelligence might help us eradicate war, disease, and poverty, and so the creation of strong AI might be the biggest event in human history. Some experts have expressed concern, though, that it might also be the last, unless we learn to align the goals of the AI with ours before it becomes superintelligent.

There are some who question whether strong AI will ever be achieved, and others who insist that the creation of superintelligent AI is guaranteed to be beneficial. At FLI we recognize both of these possibilities, but also recognize the potential for an artificial intelligence system to intentionally or unintentionally cause great harm. We believe research today will help us better prepare for and prevent such potentially negative consequences in the future, thus enjoying the benefits of AI while avoiding pitfalls.

How Can AI Be Dangerous?

Most researchers agree that a superintelligent AI is unlikely to exhibit human emotions like love or hate, and that there is no reason to expect AI to become intentionally benevolent or malevolent. Instead, when considering how AI might become a risk, experts think two scenarios most likely:

1. The AI is programmed to do something devastating: Autonomous weapons are artificial intelligence systems that are programmed to kill. In the hands of the wrong person, these weapons could easily cause mass casualties. Moreover, an AI arms race could inadvertently lead to an AI war that also results in mass casualties. To avoid being thwarted by the enemy, these weapons would be designed to be extremely difficult to simply "turn off," so humans could plausibly lose control of such a situation. This risk is one that's present even with narrow AI, but grows as levels of AI intelligence and autonomy increase.

2. The AI is programmed to do something beneficial, but it develops a destructive method for achieving its goal: This can happen whenever we fail to fully align the AI's goals with ours, which is strikingly difficult. If you ask an obedient intelligent car to take you to the airport as fast as possible, it might get you there chased by helicopters and covered in vomit, doing not what you wanted but literally what you asked for. If a superintelligent system is tasked with a ambitious geoengineering project, it might wreak havoc with our ecosystem as a side effect, and view human attempts to stop it as a threat to be met.

As these examples illustrate, the concern about advanced AI isn't malevolence but competence. A super-intelligent AI will be extremely good at accomplishing its goals, and if those goals aren't aligned with ours, we have a problem. You're probably not an evil ant-hater who steps on ants out of malice, but if you're in charge of a hydroelectric green energy project and there's an anthill in the region to be flooded, too bad for the ants. A key goal of AI safety research is to never place humanity in the position of those ants.

Why the Recent Interest in AI Safety?

Stephen Hawking, Elon Musk, Steve Wozniak, Bill Gates, and many other big names in science and technology have recently expressed concern in the media and via open letters about the risks posed by AI, joined by many leading AI researchers. Why is the subject suddenly in the headlines?

The idea that the quest for strong AI would ultimately succeed was long thought of as science fiction, centuries or more away. However, thanks to recent breakthroughs, many AI milestones, which experts viewed as decades away merely five years ago, have now been reached, making many experts take seriously the possibility of superintelligence in our lifetime. While some experts still guess that human-level AI is centuries away, most AI researchers at the 2015 Puerto Rico Conference guessed that it would happen before 2060. Since it may take decades to complete the required safety research, it is prudent to start it now.

Because AI has the potential to become more intelligent than any human, we have no surefire way of predicting how it will behave. We can't use past technological developments as much of a basis because we've never created anything that has the ability to, wittingly or unwittingly, outsmart us. The best example of what we could face may be our own evolution. People now control the planet, not because we're the strongest, fastest or biggest, but because we're the smartest. If we're no longer the smartest, are we assured to remain in control?

FLI's position is that our civilization will flourish as long as we win the race between the growing power of technology and the wisdom with which we manage it. In the case of AI technology, FLI's position is that the best way to win that race is not to impede the former, but to accelerate the latter, by supporting AI safety research.

The Top Myths About Advanced AI

A captivating conversation is taking place about the future of artificial intelligence and what it will/should mean for humanity. There are fascinating controversies where the world's leading experts disagree, such as: AI's future impact on the job market; if/when human-level AI will be developed; whether this will lead to an intelligence explosion; and whether this is something we should welcome or fear. But there are also many examples of of boring pseudo-controversies caused by people misunderstanding and talking past each other. To help ourselves focus on the interesting controversies and open questions—and not on the misunderstandings—let's clear up some of the most common myths.

Timeline Myths

The first myth regards the timeline: how long will it take until machines greatly supersede human-level intelligence? A common misconception is that we know the answer with great certainty.

One popular myth is that we know we'll get superhuman AI this century. In fact, history is full of technological over-hyping. Where are those fusion power plants and flying cars we were promised

MYTH	FACT
Superintelligence by 2100 is inevitable. Superintelligence by 2100 is impossible.	It may happen in decades, centuries, or never: AI experts disagree & we simply don't know.
Only Luddites worry about AI.	Many top AI researchers are concerned.
There is concern that AI will turn evil and/or conscious.	A more realistic concern is that AI will turn competent, with goals misaligned with ours.
Robots are the main concern.	Misaligned intelligence is the main concern: It needs no body, only an internet connection.
AI can't control humans.	Intelligence enables control: We control tigers by being smarter.
Machines can't have goals.	A heat-seeking missile has a goal.
Superintelligence is just years away.	It's at least decades away, but it may take that long to make it safe.

we'd have by now? AI has also been repeatedly over-hyped in the past, even by some of the founders of the field. For example, John McCarthy (who coined the term "artificial intelligence"), Marvin Minsky, Nathaniel Rochester and Claude Shannon wrote this overly optimistic forecast about what could be accomplished during two months with stone-age computers: "We propose that a 2 month, 10 man study of artificial intelligence be carried out during the summer of 1956 at Dartmouth College [...] An attempt will be made to find how to make machines use language, form abstractions and concepts, solve kinds of problems now reserved for humans, and improve themselves. We think that a significant advance can be made in one or more of these problems if a carefully selected group of scientists work on it together for a summer."

On the other hand, a popular counter-myth is that we know we won't get superhuman AI this century. Researchers have made a wide range of estimates for how far we are from superhuman AI, but we certainly can't say with great confidence that the probability is zero this century, given the dismal track record of such techno-skeptic predictions. For example, Ernest Rutherford, arguably the greatest nuclear physicist of his time, said in 1933—less than 24 hours before Szilard's invention of the nuclear chain reaction—that nuclear energy was "moonshine." And Astronomer Royal Richard Woolley called interplanetary travel "utter bilge" in 1956. The most extreme form of this myth is that superhuman AI will never arrive because it's physically impossible. However, physicists know that a brain consists of quarks and electrons arranged to act as a powerful computer, and that there's no law of physics preventing us from building even more intelligent quark blobs.

There have been a number of surveys asking AI researchers how many years from now they think we'll have human-level AI with at least 50% probability. All these surveys have the same conclusion: the world's leading experts disagree, so we simply don't know. For example, in such a poll of the AI researchers at the 2015 Puerto Rico AI conference, the average (median) answer was by year 2045, but some researchers guessed hundreds of years or more.

There's also a related myth that people who worry about AI think it's only a few years away. In fact, most people on record worrying about superhuman AI guess it's still at least decades away. But they argue that as long as we're not 100% sure that it won't happen this century, it's smart to start safety research now to prepare for the eventuality. Many of the safety problems associated with human-level AI are so hard that they may take decades to solve. So it's prudent to start researching them now rather than the night before some programmers drinking Red Bull decide to switch one on.

Controversy Myths

Another common misconception is that the only people harboring concerns about AI and advocating AI safety research are luddites who don't know much about AI. When Stuart Russell, author of the standard AI textbook, mentioned this during his Puerto Rico talk, the audience laughed loudly. A related misconception is that

Do Not Give Rights to Advanced Machines

Despite how human-like they may act and appear, giving rights to robots may not be the best move. That was the consensus of 150 experts who weighed in on the discussion on Thursday, in light of the European Parliament's recent question of whether or not robots need special rights.

A team of 150 experts in robotics, artificial intelligence, law, medical science and ethics wrote an open letter to the European Union advising that robots not be given special legal status as "electric persons," CNN reported. The letter says that giving robots human rights would be unhelpful.

"From an ethical and legal perspective, creating a legal personality for a robot is inappropriate whatever the legal status model," the letter states. The experts go on to claim that public perception of a robot is distorted by "Science-Fiction and a few recent sensational press announcements."

One of the reasons listed for denying robots these rights are that machines currently cannot take part in society without a human operator, and therefore cannot have their own rights. Giving a robot rights might allow an operator to claim that they are not responsible for a robot, and therefore not responsible for what a robot does.

In addition, giving a robot rights could mean that one day they must be paid for their work or given citizenship, the group says.

In addition, the letter states the benefit to humanity should preside over all the framework for any civil laws involving robots and artificial intelligence. Due to this, the protection of robot users and third parties should hold precedence in any talks about robotic rights.

The suggestion comes from an ongoing debate within Europe of whether or not to grant status to forms of artificial intelligence. The European Commission will present its initiative on artificial intelligence at the end of the month, CNN reported.

"Humans vs Robots: Don't Give Advanced Machines Rights, AI Experts Warn," by Dana Dovey, *Newsweek*, April 14, 2018.

supporting AI safety research is hugely controversial. In fact, to support a modest investment in AI safety research, people don't need to be convinced that risks are high, merely non-negligible— just as a modest investment in home insurance is justified by a non-negligible probability of the home burning down.

It may be that media have made the AI safety debate seem more controversial than it really is. After all, fear sells, and articles using out-of-context quotes to proclaim imminent doom can generate more clicks than nuanced and balanced ones. As a result, two people who only know about each other's positions from media quotes are likely to think they disagree more than they really do. For example, a techno-skeptic who only read about Bill Gates's position in a British tabloid may mistakenly think Gates believes superintelligence to be imminent. Similarly, someone in the beneficial-AI movement who knows nothing about Andrew Ng's position except his quote about overpopulation on Mars may mistakenly think he doesn't care about AI safety, whereas in fact, he does. The crux is simply that because Ng's timeline estimates are longer, he naturally tends to prioritize short-term AI challenges over long-term ones.

Myths About the Risks of Superhuman AI

Many AI researchers roll their eyes when seeing this headline: "Stephen Hawking warns that rise of robots may be disastrous for mankind." And as many have lost count of how many similar articles they've seen. Typically, these articles are accompanied by an evil-looking robot carrying a weapon, and they suggest we should worry about robots rising up and killing us because they've become conscious and/or evil. On a lighter note, such articles are actually rather impressive, because they succinctly summarize the scenario that AI researchers don't worry about. That scenario combines as many as three separate misconceptions: concern about consciousness, evil, and robots.

If you drive down the road, you have a subjective experience of colors, sounds, etc. But does a self-driving car have a subjective experience? Does it feel like anything at all to be a self-driving car? Although this mystery of consciousness is interesting in its own right, it's irrelevant to AI risk. If you get struck by a driverless car, it makes no difference to you whether it subjectively feels conscious. In the same way, what will affect us humans is what superintelligent AI does, not how it subjectively feels.

The fear of machines turning evil is another red herring. The real worry isn't malevolence, but competence. A superintelligent AI is by definition very good at attaining its goals, whatever they may be, so we need to ensure that its goals are aligned with ours. Humans don't generally hate ants, but we're more intelligent than they are—so if we want to build a hydroelectric dam and there's an anthill there, too bad for the ants. The beneficial-AI movement wants to avoid placing humanity in the position of those ants.

The consciousness misconception is related to the myth that machines can't have goals. Machines can obviously have goals in the narrow sense of exhibiting goal-oriented behavior: the behavior of a heat-seeking missile is most economically explained as a goal to hit a target. If you feel threatened by a machine whose goals are misaligned with yours, then it is precisely its goals in this narrow sense that troubles you, not whether the machine is conscious and experiences a sense of purpose. If that heat-seeking missile were chasing you, you probably wouldn't exclaim: "I'm not worried, because machines can't have goals!"

I sympathize with Rodney Brooks and other robotics pioneers who feel unfairly demonized by scaremongering tabloids, because some journalists seem obsessively fixated on robots and adorn many of their articles with evil-looking metal monsters with red shiny eyes. In fact, the main concern of the beneficial-AI movement isn't with robots but with intelligence itself: specifically, intelligence whose goals are misaligned with ours. To cause us trouble, such misaligned superhuman intelligence needs no robotic body, merely an internet connection—this may enable outsmarting financial markets, out-inventing human researchers, out-manipulating human leaders, and developing weapons we cannot even understand. Even if building robots were physically impossible, a super-intelligent and super-wealthy AI could easily pay or manipulate many humans to unwittingly do its bidding.

The robot misconception is related to the myth that machines can't control humans. Intelligence enables control: humans control tigers not because we are stronger, but because we are smarter. This means that if we cede our position as smartest on our planet, it's possible that we might also cede control.

The Interesting Controversies

Not wasting time on the above-mentioned misconceptions let us focus on true and interesting controversies where even the experts disagree. What sort of future do you want? Should we develop lethal autonomous weapons? What would you like to happen with job automation? What career advice would you give today's kids? Do you prefer new jobs replacing the old ones, or a jobless society where everyone enjoys a life of leisure and machine-produced wealth? Further down the road, would you like us to create superintelligent life and spread it through our cosmos? Will we control intelligent machines or will they control us? Will intelligent machines replace us, coexist with us, or merge with us? What will it mean to be human in the age of artificial intelligence? What would you like it to mean, and how can we make the future be that way? Please join the conversation!

> *"Overall, researchers broadly agree that current machines and robots are not conscious—in spite of a huge amount of science fiction depictions that seem to suggest otherwise."*

Consciousness Is a Key Attribute for AI Personhood

Elisabeth Hildt

In the following viewpoint, Elisabeth Hildt argues that consciousness is not currently a trait of artificial intelligence. Given that most people consider the social aspect of AI to be a key function in their existence, social interaction alone is not enough to grant AI moral personhood. Humans by comparison are granted personhood even if they do not interact socially. It is not practical to grant personhood to robots that do not have consciousness or sentience. But this could change in the future, and a discussion of what moral personhood would look like for AI is certainly warranted. Elisabeth Hildt is professor of philosophy and director of the Center for the Study of Ethics in the Professions at the Illinois Institute of Technology.

"Artificial Intelligence: Does Consciousness Matter?" *Frontiers in Psychology*, 10, 1535, by Elisabeth Hildt, Frontiers Media S.A., July 2, 2019. https://www.frontiersin.org /articles/10.3389/fpsyg.2019.01535/full. Licensed under CC BY 4.0 International.

As you read, consider the following questions:

1. What does "self-awareness" mean for artificial intelligence?
2. What is the difference between phenomenal consciousness and access consciousness?
3. Why have some authors argued for ascribing rights to artificial intelligence?

Consciousness plays an important role in debates around the mind-body problem, the controversy over strong vs. weak artificial intelligence (AI), and bioethics. Strikingly, however, it is not prominent in current debates on ethical aspects of AI and robotics. This text explores this lack and makes two claims: We need to talk more about artificial consciousness and we need to talk more about the lack of consciousness in current robots and AI.

Can Machines Have Consciousness?

The question of whether machines can have consciousness is not new, with proponents of strong artificial intelligence (strong AI) and weak AI having exchanged philosophical arguments for a considerable period of time. John R. Searle, albeit being critical toward strong AI, characterized strong AI as assuming that "… the appropriately programmed computer really is a mind, in the sense that computers given the right programs can be literally said to understand and have cognitive states" (Searle, 1980, p. 417). In contrast, weak AI assumes that machines do not have consciousness, mind and sentience but only simulate thought and understanding.

When thinking about artificial consciousness, we face several problems (Manzotti and Chella, 2018). Most fundamentally, there is the difficulty to explain consciousness, to explain how subjectivity can emerge from matter—often called the "hard problem of consciousness" (Chalmers, 1996). In addition, our understanding of human consciousness is shaped by our own phenomenal experience. Whereas, we know about human consciousness from the first-person perspective, artificial consciousness will only be accessible to us from the third-person perspective. Related to this is the question of how to know whether a machine has consciousness.

A basic assumption for artificial consciousness is that it be found in the physical world of machines and robots (Manzotti and Chella, 2018). Furthermore, any definition of artificial consciousness given by humans will have to be made from the third-person perspective, without relying on phenomenal consciousness.

One strategy is to avoid a narrow definition of machine consciousness, or to avoid giving a definition at all. An example of this strategy is given by David Levy (Levy, 2009, p. 210) who prefers to take a pragmatic view according to which it is sufficient to have a general agreement about what we mean by consciousness and suggests "let us simply use the word and get on with it."

Other authors focus on self-awareness. With regard to self-aware robots, Chatila et al. (2018, p. 1) consider relevant: "… the underlying principles and methods that would enable robots to understand their environment, to be cognizant of what they do, to take appropriate and timely initiatives, to learn from their own experience and to show that they know that they have learned and how." In contrast, Kinouchi and Mackin focus on adaptation at the system-level (Kinouchi and Mackin, 2018, p. 1), "Consciousness is regarded as a function for effective adaptation at the system-level, based on matching and organizing the individual results of the underlying parallel-processing units. This consciousness is assumed to correspond to how our mind is 'aware' when making our moment to moment decisions in our daily life."

In order to solve questions specific to artificial consciousness, it is helpful to consider the philosophical reflection around consciousness, which focuses on human (and animal) consciousness. There are many concepts of consciousness. Normally, we distinguish between (a) a conscious entity, i.e., an entity that is sentient, wakeful, has self-consciousness and subjective qualitative experiences, (b) being conscious of something, for example a rose, and (c) conscious mental states, i.e., mental states an entity is aware of being in, such as being aware of smelling a rose (Van Gulick, 2018; Gennaro, 2019).

For the discussion of artificial consciousness, Ned Block's distinction between phenomenal consciousness and access consciousness proves to be particularly helpful (Block, 1995). Whereas phenomenal consciousness relates to the experience, to what it is like to be in a conscious mental state, access consciousness refers to a mental state's availability for use by the organism, for example in reasoning and guiding behavior, and describes how a mental state is related with other mental states. The debate on artificial consciousness would clearly benefit from focusing on access consciousness.

Dehaene et al. (2017) distinguish two essential dimensions of conscious computation: global availability (C1) and self-monitoring (C2). Global availability, which they characterize as information being globally available to the organism, resembles Ned Block's access consciousness (Block, 1995). Self-monitoring (C2), which they consider as corresponding to introspection, "refers to a self-referential relationship in which the cognitive system is able to monitor its own processing and obtain information about itself" (pp. 486–487).

As the examples of approaches to define artificial consciousness given above show, different authors stress different aspects. There clearly is room for more reflection and research on what third-person definitions of artificial consciousness could look like.

Artificial Consciousness and Human-Robot Interaction

Overall, researchers broadly agree that current machines and robots are not conscious—in spite of a huge amount of science fiction depictions that seem to suggest otherwise. In a survey with 184 students, however, the answers to the question "Do you believe that contemporary electronic computers are conscious?" were: No: 82%; Uncertain: 15%; Yes: 3% (Reggia et al., 2015). Remarkably, the question in the survey was about "contemporary electronic computers," and not about AI or robots.

Consciousness-related questions may be expected to arise most easily with social robots and human-robot social interaction (Sheridan, 2016). According to a definition given by Kate Darling (Darling, 2012, p. 2), a social robot "is a physically embodied, autonomous agent that communicates and interacts with humans on a social level." Examples of social robots include MIT's Kismet, Aldebaran NAO, and the humanoid social robot Sophia by Hanson Robotics.

Social robots have several characteristics that make them special for humans: They are capable of limited decision-making and learning, can exhibit behavior, and interact with people. In addition, capabilities like nonverbal immediacy of robot social behavior (Kennedy et al., 2017), speech recognition and verbal communication (Grigore et al., 2016), facial expression, and a perceived "personality" of robots (Hendriks et al., 2011), play important roles in how humans respond to robots.

Consequently, humans tend to develop unidirectional emotional bonds with robots, project lifelike qualities, attribute human characteristics (anthropomorphizing), and ascribe intentions to social robots (Scheutz, 2011; Darling, 2012; Gunkel, 2018). A typical example, if not a culmination of this tendency, can be seen in the social humanoid robot Sophia being granted Saudi-Arabian citizenship in 2017 (Katz, 2017).

All of this raises questions concerning the status of robots, and how to respond to and interact with social robots (Gunkel, 2018). Are social robots mere things? Or are social robots quasi-agents or quasi-persons (Peter Asaro)? Socially interactive others? Quasi-others? Should robots have rights?

Even though there is a general agreement that current robots do not have sentience or consciousness, some authors (such as Coeckelbergh, 2010; Darling, 2012; Gunkel, 2018) have argued in favor of ascribing rights to robots. For example, based on research on violent behavior toward robots, Kate Darling argues that it is in line with our social values to treat robots more like pets than like mere things.

While the exact arguments in favor of ascribing rights to robots differ, what is common to these positions is that they focus on the social roles humans ascribe to robots, the relationships and emotional bonds humans build with robots, or on the social context in which humans interact with robots. They do not ascribe status based on robot capabilities but argue in favor of rights based on the role robots play for human beings.

There is a fundamental problem with this "social roles" approach, however. The suggestions it makes on how to interact with robots are not consistent with the way we interact with human beings (see also Katz, 2017). The "social roles" approach, transferred to human beings, would claim that a human being's value or rights depend strongly on his or her social roles or the interests of others. This claim would be in contradiction to the generally held view that human beings have moral status independent of their social roles. From this perspective, an entity has moral status "…if and only if it or its interests morally matter to some degree for the entity's own sake" (Jaworska and Tannenbaum, 2018).

For the ascription of status and rights to human beings, personhood is central. The concept of a person involves a number of capabilities and central themes such as rationality; consciousness; personal stance (the attitude taken toward an entity); capability of reciprocating the personal stance; verbal communication; and self-consciousness (Dennett, 1976). Daniel C. Dennett considers all of these as necessary conditions of moral personhood.

In contrast, according to the "social roles" approach, rights are being ascribed not on the basis of a robot's moral status or capabilities, but on the basis of the social roles it plays for others. This explains why consciousness does not matter for this position. For it is not plausible to claim that current robots matter morally for their own sake as long as they lack characteristics such as sentience or consciousness.

This may change in the future, however. Then it may be plausible to think about a concept of "robothood" and ascribe moral status to these future robots, based on their capabilities. There is already an interesting and controversial discussion going on about ascribing legal personhood to robots (Bryson et al., 2017; Solaiman, 2017). For the debate on the moral and legal status of robots, but also for the broader question of how to respond to and interact with machines, a better understanding of artificial consciousness, artificial rationality, artificial sentience, and similar concepts is needed. We need to talk more about artificial consciousness and the lack of consciousness in current AI and robots. In this, focusing on third-person definitions of artificial consciousness and access consciousness will prove particularly helpful.

> *"Right now, the people building AI do so with unconscious bias, limited intelligence and are frequently driven by personal gain rather than the welfare of others."*

Artificial Intelligence May Be More Humane Than People

John Holden

In the following viewpoint, John Holden takes issue with the idea that advanced artificial intelligence will somehow lead to world destruction. Holden argues that humans know how to solve many issues that plague nations and peoples, yet they often ignore solutions because they may inhibit a natural human tendency toward greed and power. How do we know that machines won't do a better job at tackling chronic human issues if they are programmed to be dispassionate and objective? To this point in history, Holden argues, humans have lived in a state of organized chaos. Perhaps AI can do better. John Holden is a freelance writer specializing in science, technology, and innovation.

"Artificial Intelligence May Be More Humane Than People," by John Holden, the *Irish Times*, April 26, 2018. Reprinted by permission.

As you read, consider the following questions:

1. How and why does the author cite Elon Musk at the beginning and end of the viewpoint?
2. Why does Holden use an Ikea chair as a metric for artificial intelligence?
3. What is Holden's opinion of organized religion as a way to keep humans in check?

Artificial Intelligence (AI) appears to be suffering from an image crisis. Many of the most vocal commentators seem to believe it will ultimately cause more harm than good. While fear of new technology is nothing new, it doesn't help when thought leaders like Elon Musk join the prophets of doom. But guess what? Sometimes even Elon Musk is wrong. There I said it.

I struggled to find consensus on an antonym for AI. So we're calling it natural intelligence. That is, the stuff that's supposed to be crammed into our brains making us top of the food chain. But it's overrated. And the fact that so many have blindly concluded AI will be the death of civilisation as we know it is one part humanity's inclination to fear the unknown, and three parts *The Terminator* movies. Thanks Arnie.

If AI does learn how to self-evolve and, therefore, think for itself, who is to say it wouldn't develop consciousness that was genuinely altruistic, compassionate and fair-minded? Right now, the people building AI do so with unconscious bias, limited intelligence and are frequently driven by personal gain rather than the welfare of others. That's why the greatest achievements have come from corporate entities like Facebook, who use it for targeted advertising, photo tagging and news feeds. Microsoft and Apple need AI to make their digital assistants, Cortana and Siri, wow us by turning on the immersion.

Google is by far one of the hardest at work in its efforts to create the kind of self-teaching AI that might one day outsmart us all. It recently promoted one of its own whizz kids to be the new lead of its AI division. While not a kid at 50 years of age, Jeff Dean had been impressing his co-workers at Google with his robotics skills since 1999. So he was an obvious choice.

Machine-Driven Apocalypse

A position like this at a company like Google isn't one of those "made-up" titles like vice-president of customer development or chief innovation officer. AI strategy is at the heart of everything the company does. So if anyone is to inadvertently cause a machine-driven apocalypse, it'll be these guys.

We're not there yet though. AI's greatest screw-ups have also come from the corporate sector. In 2015, Google's photo-organising product tagged some images of black people as gorillas.

News that a robot figured out how to autonomously assemble an Ikea chair without malfunctioning, like most humans do, is kind of impressive. But it's not enough to run screaming to the hills. Researchers at Nanyang Technological University in Singapore used a couple of bog standard industrial robot arms with force sensors and a 3D camera to build a robot that had a Stefan Ikea chair assembled in 20 minutes.

It was programmed to build the chair. It knew no other option than this. So given the choice, would a conscious machine decide not to help a human in distress assemble a chair? No one is wildly speculating on the possibility that robots that can think for themselves might choose to be altruistic, compassionate and fair. That they might protect the most vulnerable in society, distribute wealth equally, and put criminal, narcissistic, incompetent leaders of the free world, for example, into recovery treatment rather than a jail cell which is what humans would consider doing first.

Machines vs Myopia

There are already solutions to many of the world's ills—wealth inequality, environmental damage, racial and cultural discrimination etc—at our disposal. We as a species choose not to implement them because of the potential negative impacts—

financial loss, time-consumption, not to mention apathy—they might have on us as individuals in the short term. Machines might not be so myopic.

Of course, taking a cold, rational approach to decision-making isn't necessarily the best idea for society's ills either. The debate really centres around what we constitute as consciousness. Can a robot develop a sense of itself—and of those around it—while continuing to deliver a purely logic-based approach to "choice"? Were this the case, artificial decision-making could decide eugenics is back in vogue.

All humans have managed to achieve thus far though is a kind of organised chaos. People will stop at a red light and wait till it's green before driving through an intersection. But in the back of everyone's mind is the knowledge that it would take very little for civil society to fall apart and have us all at each other's throats. That's why so many take comfort in organised religion as it offers answers to many of our questions. They might not be the right answers but sometimes living a lie is easier than accepting the harsh reality that we have little or no control over our lives.

From what I can tell, machines aren't big on chaos either. They prefer order, logic and fully formed Ikea chairs. At a recent talk he gave in Austin, Texas, Elon Musk said, "Smart people who know they're smart have a tendency to define themselves by their intelligence meaning they don't like the idea that machines could ever be smarter than them." I'm no psychologist but Musk himself happens to be a smart man who is clearly aware of his own intelligence. The engineer doth protest too much, methinks.

Periodical and Internet Sources Bibliography

The following articles have been selected to supplement the diverse views presented in this chapter.

Janna Anderson and Lee Rainee, "Artificial Intelligence and the Future of Humans," Pew Research Center, December 10, 2018. https://www.pewresearch.org/internet/2018/12/10/artificial -intelligence-and-the-future-of-humans/

Janosch Delcker, "Europe Divided over Robot 'Personhood,'" Politico, April 11, 2018. https://www.politico.eu/article/europe-divided -over-robot-ai-artificial-intelligence-personhood/

Luke Dormehl, "I, Alexa: Should We Give Artificial Intelligence Human Rights?" Digital Trends, July 5, 2017. https://www .digitaltrends.com/cool-tech/ai-personhood-ethics-questions/

Nick Eason, "Rights for Robots: Why We Need Better AI Regulation," *Raconteur*, October 16, 2019. https://www.raconteur.net/risk -management/legal-innovation-2019/robot-rights-ethics

Tyler L. Janes, "Legal Personhood for Artificial Intelligence: Citizenship as the Exception to the Rule," *AI & Society*, vol. 35, pp. 343–354, 2020. https://link.springer.com /article/10.1007/s00146-019-00897-9

Kristin Manganello, "Defining Personhood in the Age of AI," Thomas, November 15, 2018. https://www.thomasnet.com /insights/defining-personhood-in-the-age-of-ai/

Carlos E. Perez, "Artificial Personhood Is the Root Cause Why A.I. Is Dangerous to Society," Medium, March 21, 2018. https://medium .com/intuitionmachine/the-dangers-of-artificial-intelligence-is -unavoidable-due-to-flaws-of-human-civilization-f9c131e65e5e

Mathias Risse, "Human Rights and Artificial Intelligence: An Urgently Needed Agenda," Carr Center for Human Rights Policy, May 2018. https://carrcenter.hks.harvard.edu/files/cchr/files /humanrightsai_designed.pdf

Dan Robitzski, "You Have No Idea What Artificial Intelligence Really Does," Futurism, October 16, 2016. https://futurism.com /artificial-intelligence-hype

Jamie Rollo, "Artificial Intelligence and Personhood: The Moral Conundrum," *Bleu Magazine,* September 23, 2019. https://www.bleumag.com/2019/09/23/artificial-intelligence-and-personhood-the-moral-conundrum/

Daniel Schlaepfer and Hugo Kruyne, "AI and Robots Should Not Be Attributed Legal Personhood," Euractiv, March 26, 2018. https://www.euractiv.com/section/economy-jobs/opinion/ai-and-robots-should-not-be-attributed-legal-personhood/

Natalie Wolchover, "Artificial Intelligence Will Do What We Ask. That's a Problem," *Quanta Magazine*, January 30, 2020. https://www.quantamagazine.org/artificial-intelligence-will-do-what-we-ask-thats-a-problem-20200130/

For Further Discussion

Chapter 1

1. Can you create a definition of personhood for the twenty-first century, taking into account all of the various humans, corporations, and inanimate objects that may qualify for the designation?
2. After reading viewpoints by Doris Lin and Steven M. Wise, do you favor animal personhood?
3. Is there an ecological benefit to according personhood to rivers, lakes, and other natural bodies?

Chapter 2

1. After reading the viewpoints in this chapter, how do you feel about *Citizens United* and corporate personhood?
2. Does granting personhood to corporations diminish the idea of personhood for humans?
3. Does corporate personhood create an uneven playing field when it comes to money in politics? Why or why not?

Chapter 3

1. After reading the viewpoints in this chapter, does the notion of personhood for the unborn add anything substantive to the abortion debate or is it just a new way to say the same thing?
2. Does personhood for the fetus endanger maternal personhood?
3. How do you feel about the notion that those who favor fetal rights must also be equally supportive of children's rights after birth? Why?

Chapter 4

1. After reading the viewpoints in this chapter, do you believe AI should have legal personhood?
2. Is granting personhood for AI merely a way of absolving manufacturers from legal trouble should their creations go awry?
3. Many of the issues in this chapter have been dealt with in science fiction, from *I, Robot* to *Blade Runner*. Is such fiction a valuable way of confronting truth? Why or why not?

Organizations to Contact

The editors have compiled the following list of organizations concerned with the issues debated in this book. The descriptions are derived from materials provided by the organizations. All have publications or information available for interested readers. The list was compiled on the date of publication of the present volume; the information provided here may change. Be aware that many organizations take several weeks or longer to respond to inquiries, so allow as much time as possible.

American Civil Liberties Union (ACLU)

125 Broad Street
New York, NY 10004-2400
(212) 549-2500
website: www.aclu.org

The ACLU considers itself to be the nation's guardian of liberty, working in courts, legislatures, and communities to defend and preserve the individual rights and liberties that the Constitution and the laws of the United States guarantee. Among the issues they focus on are human rights, racial equality, and women's rights.

American Enterprise Institute for Public Policy Research (AEI)

1789 Massachusetts Avenue NW
Washington, DC 20036
(202) 862-5800
email: tyler.castle@aei.org
website: www.aei.org

The American Enterprise Institute is a conservative public policy think tank that sponsors original research on the world economy, US foreign policy and international security, and domestic political and social issues. AEI is dedicated to defending human dignity, expanding human potential, and building a freer and safer world.

The Association for the Advancement of Artificial Intelligence (AAAI)

2275 East Bayshore Road, Suite 160
Palo Alto, CA 94303
(650) 328-3123
website: www.aaai.org

The Association for the Advancement of Artificial Intelligence (AAAI) is a nonprofit scientific society devoted to advancing the scientific understanding of the mechanisms underlying thought and intelligent behavior and their embodiment in machines. AAAI aims to promote research in, and responsible use of, artificial intelligence.

Cato Institute

1000 Massachusetts Avenue NW
Washington, DC 20001-5403
(202) 842-0200
website: www.cato.org

The Cato Institute is a libertarian public policy research organization, a think tank dedicated to the principles of individual liberty, limited government, free markets, and peace. Its scholars and analysts conduct independent research on a wide range of policy issues. Articles include "Privacy Rights and 'Corporate Personhood,'" "So What If Corporations Aren't People?" and "When Does a Baby Become a Person?"

ConservAmerica

1455 Pennsylvania Avenue NW
Suite 400
Washington, DC 20004
email: info@conservamerica.org
website: www.conservamerica.org

ConservAmerica is a nonprofit organization dedicated to the development and advancement of sound environmental and conservation policy. ConservAmerica believes in the protection and preservation of the United States' national heritage through sound public policy that leverages private investment, embraces local solutions, and spurs innovation. It considers conservation that protects the environment and the economy to be a bipartisan endeavor.

Environmental Defense Fund (EDF)

1875 Connecticut Avenue NW
Suite 600
Washington, DC 20009
(202) 572-3298
website: www.edf.org

The Environmental Defense Fund is one of the world's leading environmental organizations. In the US, *Fortune* magazine called its board one of the country's most influential nonprofit boards. Science continues to guide all of EDF's policies. Its searchable database contains numerous links to articles concerning environmental science and the protection of nature.

National Organization for Women (NOW)

1100 H Street NW, 3rd Floor
Washington, DC 20005
(202) 628-8669
email: www.now.org/about/contact-us/
website: www.now.org

The National Organization for Women considers itself to be the grassroots arm of the women's movement and is dedicated to its multi-issue and multi-strategy approach to women's rights. NOW's purpose is to take action to promote feminist ideals, lead societal change, eliminate discrimination, and achieve and protect the equal rights of all women and girls in all aspects of social, political, and economic life.

National Right to Life

1446 Duke Street
Alexandria, VA 22314
(202) 626-8800
email: education@nrlc.org
website: www.nrlc.org

The aim of National Right to Life is to protect and defend what it considers to be the most fundamental right of humankind, the right to life of every human being from the beginning of life to natural death. National Right to Life carries out its mission by promoting respect for the worth and dignity of every individual human being, born or unborn, including unborn children from their beginning; those newly born; persons with disabilities; older people; and other vulnerable people, especially those who cannot defend themselves.

National Women's Law Center (NWLC)

11 Dupont Circle NW, #800
Washington, DC 20036
(202) 588-5180
website: www. nwlc.org

The National Women's Law Center fights for gender justice in court, in public policy, and in society. It focuses on issues that are central to the lives of women and girls. It uses legal means to change culture and drive solutions to the gender inequity that shapes our society and to break down barriers. It especially aids those who face multiple forms of discrimination, including women of color, LGBTQ people, and low-income women and families.

Sierra Club

2101 Webster Street, Suite 1300
Oakland, CA 94612
(415) 977-5500
email: information@sierraclub.org
website: www.sierraclub.org

The Sierra Club is an influential grassroots environmental organization dedicated to defending everyone's right to a healthy world. Its concerns include global warming, unprecedented levels of pollution, and powerful special interests undermining basic environmental protections. Its website includes information on protections for natural resources, climate change, and other current environmental issues.

US Commission on Civil Rights (USCCR)

1331 Pennsylvania Avenue NW, Suite 1150
Washington, DC 20425
(202) 376-7700
website: www.usccr.gov

The USCCR's mission is to inform the development of national civil rights policy and enhance enforcement of federal civil rights laws. It pursues this mission by studying alleged deprivations of voting rights and alleged discrimination based on race, color, religion, sex, age, disability, or national origin, or in the administration of justice.

Bibliography of Books

M. Ryan Calo, Michael Froomkin, and Ian Kerr. *Robot Law.* Cheltenham, UK: Edward Elgar Publishing Limited, 2016.

Alasdair Cochrane. *Should Animals Have Political Rights?* Medford, MA: Polity, 2020.

Marcelo Corrales, Mark Fenwick, and Nikolaus Forgó. *Robotics, AI and the Future of Law.* Singapore: Springer, 2018.

Olivia Dee. *The Anti-Abortion Campaign in England, 1966-1989.* New York, NY: Routledge, 2020.

Jay Friedenberg. *The Future of the Self: An Interdisciplinary Approach to Personhood and Identity in the Digital Age.* Oakland, CA: University of California Press, 2020.

Joshua C. Gellers. *Rights for Robots: Artificial Intelligence, Animal, and Environmental Law.* New York, NY: Routledge, 2021.

Juli L. Gittinger. *Personhood in Science Fiction: Religious and Philosophical Considerations.* Cham, Switzerland: Palgrave Macmillan, 2019.

Jody Greene and Sharif Youssef. *Human Rights After Corporate Personhood.* Toronto, ON: University of Toronto Press, 2020.

Christopher Hutton. *Integrationism and the Self: Reflections on the Legal Personhood of Animals.* New York, NY: Taylor & Francis Group, 2019.

Lindsey N. Kingston. *Fully Human: Personhood, Citizenship, and Rights.* New York, NY: Oxford University Press, 2019.

Visa A. J. Kurki. *A Theory of Legal Personhood.* Oxford, UK: Oxford University Press, 2019.

Cameron La Follette and Chris Maser. *Sustainability and the Rights of Nature in Practice*. Boca Raton, FL: CRC Press, 2020.

Antonia Lolordo. *Persons: A History*. New York, NY: Oxford University Press, 2019.

Bertha Alvarez Manninen and Jack Mulder Jr. *Civil Dialogue on Abortion*. London, UK: Taylor and Francis, 2018.

Tomasz Pietrzykowski and Krystyna Warchał. *Personhood Beyond Humanism: Animals, Chimeras, Autonomous Agents and the Law*. Cham, Switzerland: Springer, 2018.

Gregory F. Tague. *An Ape Ethic and the Question of Personhood*. Blue Ridge Summit, PA: Rowman & Littlefield, 2020.

Tamara Thompson. *Abortion*. Farmington Hills, MI: Greenhaven Press, 2015.

Adam Winkler. *We the Corporations: How American Businesses Won Their Civil Rights*. New York, NY: Liveright Publishing Corporation, 2019.

Index

Y